Spiritual Masters
SAI BABA

THE SERIES

The Spiritual Masters series is intended to serve as a first reader on the lives and teachings of some of the Masters who have enriched our life on this planet. They created a sublime body of knowledge, using such diverse means as song and silence to communicate their wisdom. They arose at different points in history, in diverse cultural and social contexts, yet they all spoke the language of love and compassion.

In today's troubled times, when people are getting increasingly divided along religious lines, the message of these Teachers assumes greater relevance. This series attempts to reach out to the modern reader by presenting the Master and his teaching in a simple, narrative format.

The Buddha and Sai Baba are the first two titles in this series. Subsequent titles would include Sant Dnyaneshwar, Adi Sankara, Mahavira, Moses, Jesus, Zarathustra, Kabir, Meerabai, Guru Nanak and Khwaja Moinuddin Chishti.

More information available at: www.indussource.com
email: info@indussource.com

Spiritual Masters
SAI BABA

Sonavi Desai

Indus Source Books

Smriti Books

ISBN: 81-87967-64-1

First Edition : 2003
Reprint :   2004

Copyright © Sonavi Desai 2003
Second Revised Edition 2004
Cover Design copyright © Indus Source

Co-Published by:

Indus Source Books
PO Box 6194
Malabar Hill PO
Mumbai 400 006
INDIA

Smriti Books
124 Siddarth Enclave
New Delhi 110 014
INDIA

Printed at
Excel Printers Pvt. Ltd.
C- 206, Naraina Industrial Area, Phase-I
New Delhi 110028

This book is sold subject to the condition that it shall not by way of trade or otherwise, be lent, resold, hired out, or otherwise circulated without the publisher's prior written consent in any form of binding or cover other than that in which it is published and without a similar condition including this condition being imposed on the subsequent purchaser and without limiting the rights under copyright reserved above, no part of this publication may be reproduced, stored in a retrieval system, or transmitted in any form, or by any means, electronic, mechanical, photocopying, recording or otherwise, without the prior written permission of both the copyright owner and the above-mentioned publishers of this book.

For my parents

Acknowledgements

I would like to thank:

My children Antara and Agastya for sowing the seeds of this work and for their unconditional appreciation of its contents.

My parents and my husband Anand for their support and patient reading of the manuscript as it progressed.

Shri M.V. Kamath for writing a foreword and for all the words of encouragement.

Shri Sitaram Dhanu who made time for a most informative visit to Shirdi.

Shri C.V. Dabholkar and Shri Pandurang Tukaram alias Bhai Humne who have kindly given me access to some rare photographs.

Gouri Dange for her valuable inputs during the editing of this book.

My friend and partner Supriya Rai for all the serious discussions, heated debates and moments of laughter during the ups and downs of this venture.

FOREWORD

Of all the countries of the world India with its hoary civilisation undoubtedly is the luckiest. For centuries it has given birth to a tradition of saints who have enriched the times in which they lived, bringing hope and succour to their devotees. Among them is Sai Baba of Shirdi.

Sai Baba is a phenomenon. In all of India's long and shining history there has never been anyone like him. He is not a conventional saint. As I have written in another context, he had no pretensions to sainthood. He addressed no audiences. He wrote no tomes. Once he made the then insignificant hamlet Shirdi his home, he never stirred out. He initiated no disciple to take over from him. Yes, he performed 'miracles' but in no manner of means to impress anyone. What others were accustomed to describe as miracles came naturally to him. Sai Baba was just being himself. A man of God. An *avatar*.

Of course he spoke with authority. He could say in utter simplicity: "Wherever you go, I am always with you. I dwell in your heart. Do not regard yourself as separate from me. We are one." And those who had come to know him and adored him knew that every word was true. Sai Baba was to them their father and mother, friend and philosopher, someone they could turn to in times of distress.

Sai Baba came from Marathwada, the home of Maharashtra's medieval saints. Born in Pathri, about twenty years before the Sepoy Mutiny of 1857, he was to make his permanent home in Shirdi. It speaks for the power of his spirituality that today his name is a household word in many parts of the world. He is with them who love him. He is with them wherever they are.

Countless stories about his life and work are now part of the Sai heritage and many of them have been recorded. Even so they are not readily available to the young. It is this lacuna that is sought to be filled by Sonavi Desai.

Each chapter is complete in itself. Each records a story rich in meaning and significance. This book presents Sai Baba in all his munificence, love and care. Reading it brings Sai Baba closer to the reader. His divine presence is actually *felt*. Time stops.

Such a book had long been needed to be written if only to present to a generation coming of age India's rich and abundant heritage.

Baba once said – and it is recorded in this book: "In whatever faith men worship me, even so do I render to them. Know that my eye is ever on those who love me". It may sound strange to a generation brought up on Harry Potter. But to have faith is to live and live well.

What is so special about this work is its essential readability. Its sensitivity. Its awareness. Its 'with-it'ness.

Foreword

By presenting Baba in the shape of a dialogue between grandma and her grandchildren the author provides a human touch. Words are transformed effortlessly into feelings, emotions.

The children – Narsimha, Saraswati, Kashinath – could be us. Any of us. All of us. Waiting to hear about Baba, wishing to be in his eternal presence.

The writing is effortless, straight from the heart. And therefore, heart-warming. May this work touch the hearts of the readers and water their faith as much in Baba as in themselves for their own good and the good of the world.

M. V. Kamath
Mumbai
March 2003

A photograph of Baba taken against his will.
Baba appears as a blurred silhouette under the umbrella.

INTRODUCTION

"Let no man in the world live in delusion. Without a Guru none can cross over to the other shore"
~ Guru Nanak

This book started out as a collection of stories for my own children. They would often ask me to narrate some stories of Baba. Their obvious delight in listening to the fascinating tales from his life encouraged me to put pen to paper.

'Spiritual Masters – Sai Baba' has been a labour of love and devotion, holding a wealth of meaning and sentiment. It is a very small expression of gratitude for some wonderful experiences that have enriched my life.

Sai Baba of Shirdi is one of the most well known Spiritual Masters of India. He belongs to that brotherhood of saints who crossed the barriers of caste and creed and spoke the universal language of love. He conveyed his message through words, action and visions. Profound philosophy is not within the grasp of all but Baba explained it in a simple and forthright way. He fulfilled his mission on earth and touched the lives of millions of people.

Baba's origins are unknown – he did not disclose where he came from. Like Kabir, he chose not to classify himself as either Hindu or Muslim. He believed in the oneness of humanity and the equality of all religions. He encouraged people to worship according to their own faith and to respect the beliefs and faith of others as well. In today's world of intolerance and strife, Baba's teachings gain even more significance.

Baba never wrote any spiritual treatise nor did he leave behind any successor. His life itself revealed the greatest Truth. He had acquired the highest level of Consciousness and his devotees experienced his miraculous powers.

People today are sceptical of the concept of miracles; their belief in rational thinking often brings this phenomenon under attack. By its very nature, a miracle defies natural laws and is therefore unacceptable to a logical mind. The stories narrated in this book revolve around the wonder of Baba's 'miraculous' powers and are sometimes loosely termed 'miracles'. However, Baba, like other true spiritual Masters, never 'performed' miracles – they manifested themselves naturally as one aspect of his unique spirituality.

What exactly is a miracle? It is an extraordinary event contrary to the laws of nature, attributed to a divine power. It is a supernatural phenomenon, which is the result of a very active spiritual consciousness, which manifests itself, transcending time and space. A person in this state of heightened consciousness is able to reach the inner consciousness of others.

What is perceived by people to be a miracle is, in fact, a logical occurrence for a person who lives in the realm of the spirit. It seems out of the ordinary only to those who do not have an insight into the workings of cosmic creation. Therefore, when Baba 'miraculously' cured or saved a devotee, it was purely a natural manifestation of his powers. It stemmed from a plane where sensory pain or pleasure did not exist. As Swami Rama writes, "When individual consciousness expands itself to cosmic consciousness, it becomes easy to feel delight in suffering for the sake of others. For him, it is not suffering, though ordinary people feel he is suffering."

The basis of miracles is faith. To one who has faith, no explanation of miracles is necessary and to one who has no faith, no explanation is possible. Miracles have always been experienced by persons who believe – miracles are a response to faith.

Great Masters like Jesus and Sai Baba, without consciously willing it, have revealed this aspect of their spirituality, either to cure physical diseases or to awaken people to the consciousness of God. As Baba has said, "I give people what they want in the hope that they will begin to want what I want to give them." This subtle yet powerful message underlies the tales told herein.

Baba's life before he appeared in Shirdi as a young man is not known. This book therefore does not purport to be a biography. It is a collection of stories from his life portrayed through the eyes of Laxmi, one of his closest devotees. While material facts have been kept intact, an element of fiction has been introduced to weave events from his life into a narrative. The stories in this book have been recounted with the hope that Baba's teachings will reaffirm our faith in peace, tolerance and universal love.

CONTENTS

Foreword	ix
Introduction	xiii
Dassera, 1918	1
The Discovery	6
One of Us	13
Construction of Buti's Wada	21
Lights Burned without Oil	26
And the Well Overflowed...	34
Who was Baba's Guru?	41
Sufi Synthesis	48
The Vanishing Tongawallah	54
Baba's Invisible Hand	61
I am the River Ganga	65
The Magic Dishes	69
A Dream Come True	73
Baba Proves the Astrologer Wrong	79
Saved from the Flames	82
Back from the Dead	85
Distance is No Barrier	89
Compassion	93
An Heir for Ratanji	98
I have Many Forms	103
Sister Act	109
The Frog and the Serpent	112
Sanyasi or Sai?	121
Chor-Police	127

God is One	133
Telepathy	140
Knowledge	145
Plagued by Cholera	151
The Tale of Two Pilgrims	156
Wisdom from a Child	163
Grace of the Guru	167
The Vision	172
Epilogue	179
Glossary	185
Researching the Origins	191

DASSERA, 1918

Today is Dassera. It is Tuesday, the 15th of October 1918. It would normally have been a day to celebrate and rejoice. An end to the nine days of fasting and penance during Navratri. But today there is only one thought that reverberates through my mind : Baba is no more. Baba has attained *samadhi* and left his physical body on this auspicious day. No more will I see him in Dwarkamai, talking, smiling, beckoning. Shirdi feels bereft, without the familiar, reassuring figure of Baba.

I make my way out into the courtyard and sit on the *khaat*, a rope cot. It is dusk and the sky is awash in shades of pink and orange. So many times I have sat thus of an evening with Baba in Dwarkamai, the atmosphere filled with a sense of peace and fulfillment.

Tears spring to my eyes. Will there ever be another like him? Who will be our refuge now? Who will bring peace to all those suffering people? I know that Baba's spirit will always live on. He has promised to come to us even after giving up the physical body. But I, who have known him since childhood, find it very hard indeed to accept that I will not see him in flesh and blood anymore. Baba was my Guru, yes, but he was so much, much more too. He was my friend and my guide and my parent all rolled into one. Quite simply, he was my world in its entirety.

The events leading to Baba's *samadhi* pass through my mind. It was expected, but all the same, reality is often very hard to accept. A world without Baba was unthinkable.

Baba had been unwell for a few days. He was running a fever and had become quite weak. It hurt us all to see him in this condition. Somewhere, deep within, we knew that his time to depart was drawing near. But we didn't want to even think of it, we just wanted him to recover. Every sign of improvement gave us a new surge of hope. Wishing to be by Baba's side as much as possible, I had taken to spending all my free moments with him. Today was no different. This morning, I had as usual taken *bhakris* and vegetable for Baba. All his devotees were sitting around, lovingly waiting upon him. I sat in a corner, watching him, trying to imprint that dear face on my mind forever. His body was no longer that of the strapping young man who had come to Shirdi so many years ago. His face now had wrinkles, his gait was slower and his hair underneath the head-cloth was sparse and grey. Yet, his eyes were just the same. Lustrous, mesmerizing eyes, full of love and kindness, and shining with some divine light.

After a while, Baba shakily stood up. He looked very calm and composed. He then quietly asked most of the people around to go for lunch. Nobody wanted to leave Baba at this critical time.

"Go," Baba insisted, "you must eat." Remaining with Baba were a handful of devotees – Shama, Bayaji Kote-Patil, Nimonkar, Bhagoji and myself.

After the others had left, he called us closer.

Dassera, 1918

"Come and sit by me," he said, sitting down again in his favourite spot in Dwarkamai. He closed his eyes and seemed to be in deep meditation. We sat with him in silence. We sat thus for a while basking in the presence of this truly astounding spirit, each of us immersed in our own thoughts about him.

All of a sudden, Baba called out to me. Surprised, I tremulously stepped up to him. Putting his hand in the pocket of his *kafni*, he pulled out nine silver rupee coins. He handed me first five and then four. Full of emotion, unable to speak, I only held out my hand. Somewhere at the back of my mind, I was trying to understand the significance of what Baba was doing. He often communicated in riddles, in a manner that made sense only to the person he was addressing. My thoughts were in a whirl, deciphering the coded language of the nine rupees. Always remember the *Ninefold Path to Devotion and Salvation*, Baba seemed to indicate. I could not utter a word. I just looked at him, my brimming eyes conveying my answer. "I promise, Baba, I will."

Everyone was now crowding around Baba. It seemed that all at once the atmosphere in Dwarkamai had changed. There was an intangible feeling of unease. A feeling that one could only sense, that I cannot put into words. The seconds seemed to be ticking by faster now.

Nimonkar tried to give Baba some water but it spilt out of his mouth. "Take me to the Wada," said Baba in a feeble voice. And then within seconds, before anyone could grasp what was happening, he had gone. It was all over. He had left his physical body and merged with the Eternal. He had accomplished his purpose on earth and was called back to the realm of the perfect yogis.

Tears flow freely from my eyes as I think of Baba. In my hand I still clutch the nine coins that Baba gave me today. They are precious to me now. Precious, for having come to me from Baba's own hand. Precious, for symbolising Baba's teachings. Oh Baba, I think, as sob after sob wracks my body, how will I bear not seeing you again? How will I ever climb the steps to an empty Dwarkamai?

Memories of Baba are all I shall have left to live with. I feel like I shall never roast another *bhakri* without feeling a stab of pain. There is no Baba to feed anymore... It has been my daily routine, ever since I can remember, to roast *bhakris* for Baba and take them to Dwarkamai. He would be waiting for me with a smile, not having eaten a morsel of food. I would crush them and mix them in milk and he would happily eat them. Now that too will be just a memory. I remember the rare occasions when I was late. I would rush to Dwarkamai, feeling totally wretched, knowing that Baba would be hungry. He would be waiting patiently, uncomplaining.

"You should have eaten something Baba, you must be hungry," I would admonish him.

"What? Eat something else when you have prepared those *bhakris* for me with so much love?" he would answer gently.

Sometimes I would take him vermicelli *kheer* in the afternoon. How he enjoyed eating it! I would sit by him and watch with satisfaction as the bowl was emptied...

My tears do not seem to stop. Will this heaviness in my heart ever be lifted? I wonder. I open the palm of my hand and look at the nine silver coins. I feel special that Baba had chosen me for his last act of grace. In his last moments he was conveying a final message to me. He was reminding me of the *Ninefold Path of Devotion and Conduct*. I must follow his teachings, I tell myself. I must be worthy of him. That will be my ultimate tribute to him. To remember his words and carry out his wishes. Baba always said, "Be free of greed, jealousy, anger and grief. Do your duty without attachment. Centre your mind and strive to walk on the spiritual path. Do not be swayed by happiness or sorrow."

I clutch the nine rupees tightly in my hand. I take a deep breath. "I will live by what you have taught me Baba," I whisper aloud, wiping the tears from my eyes. There is a sudden, gentle breeze, carrying away my words on its wings....

THE DISCOVERY

The sound of squeals and shouts greets my ears. I can see my neighbour's children playing in the common courtyard that I share with them. But it is not the usual carefree merriment I hear. Sensing the air of sadness all around, they too seem to have lost some of their normal zest.

"Narsimha, Saru, Kashi, dinnertime," I hear their mother Janki call.

"Coming Aai," answers Narsimha, the oldest at eight, as he herds his younger siblings into the house. They are lovely children and we share a special bond. I find a lot of joy in their company and to them I am 'Aji', their adopted grandmother, who tells them stories and lets them get away with murder. They spend a lot of time in my home, secretly enjoying special treats which their mother does not always allow them to indulge in.

I continue sitting in the courtyard, gazing at the stars, which have suddenly spread out like a carpet in the sky. Soon the children come out and head over to where I sit.

"Were you crying, Aji? Why?" asks Saraswati perceptively.

"Because Baba is no more, Saru," explains Narsimha patiently to his sister. "Aji, tell us more about Baba. Tell us again how he appeared in Shirdi."

"Yes Aji, tell us the story of the mare," pipes up Kashinath, clambering into my lap.

"Tell us about Baba......" Baba. Yes, there is so much to tell and yet I don't know where to begin. These children have not been as fortunate as I, who have lived in the presence of Baba all my life. I desperately want to convey to them who and what Baba really was. But is that possible? I can only tell them in my limited way, about his wonderful *leelas*, his saintliness and his compassion.

"Alright, I will tell you the story of how Baba came to Shirdi with Chand Patil of Dhoop." Cuddling Kashinath's warm, chubby body in my arms, I begin.

"It was a hot day, about sixty summers ago. Chand Patil walked through the woods towards his village of Dhoop, looking very dejected. The furrows on his forehead, deepened with worry, made him look older than his 30 years. The merry chirping of the birds and the gurgling of the water as it gushed down the stream held no charm for him that day. He pondered his misfortune, wondering what he ought to do next. It was two months since Chand Patil had lost his mare while travelling to Aurangabad. He had searched high and low for her but in vain. Finally, feeling totally depressed he had decided to give up the search.

As Chand Patil sadly made his way home he came upon a young man sitting at the foot of a tree, smoking a *chillum*.

The man was dressed like a *fakir*. He wore a *kafni* and had a white scarf tied around his head. As Chand Patil passed him, the *fakir* shouted, 'Hello, what is the matter?'

'I have lost my mare,' replied Chand Patil morosely.

'Well, why don't you look for her by the *nala* nearby?' said the *fakir* casually, without looking up.

Chand Patil was a bit taken aback. What would this *fakir* smoking a pipe know about his mare? After all, hadn't he searched for her everywhere? Without having any real hope of finding her by the *nala*, Chand Patil went to have a look anyway. Imagine his astonishment on seeing his mare calmly grazing there, almost as though she was waiting for him!

She neighed contentedly on seeing her master, coming up to nuzzle against his shoulder. Chand Patil was overcome with wonderment. This was indeed a miracle! He rushed back to the *fakir* to thank him.

The *fakir* was still calmly smoking his clay pipe. As Chand Patil stood before him, he said, 'Would you like to smoke?' His voice was deep and low.

Chand Patil nodded his head. Thereupon the *fakir* started to prepare a clay pipe for him. Realizing that there was no water to wet the pipe or fire to light it, Chand Patil offered to fetch both for the *fakir*. The *fakir* only stared at him for a moment. Then, to Chand Patil's utter amazement, he hit the ground with a baton and out came a spray of water. And then, as Chand Patil watched, the *fakir* thrust a pair of tongs into the ground and drew out a burning ember. Chand Patil noticed how long his arms were, reaching well below his knees.

Chand Patil could not believe his eyes. He looked at the *fakir*, still so calm and composed. He found himself mesmerized by the *fakir*'s eyes. They were large and dark and very bright. His face had a glow and a beautiful serene expression. He was of average height and fairly well built. 'Such a young lad,' thought Chand Patil to himself, 'but whence this air of great wisdom at such a tender age?'

He is an *aulia*, a holy man, decided Chand Patil.

The *fakir* was puffing on his *chillum*. 'Why do you stand? Be seated,' he said to Chand Patil. He then handed over the prepared *chillum* to him. Chand Patil hesitantly took a puff. He watched the *fakir* from the corner of his eye. He was gazing into the distance, a look of contemplation on his face.

'Where is your home, respected Sir?' Chand Patil summoned up the courage to ask. The *fakir* turned to give him an assessing look. 'The world is my home,' he said enigmatically, indicating the vast expanse of earth and sky with a wave of his hand.

'Then pray, come with me to my humble abode,' said Chand Patil. 'My sister is soon to be married to a boy in Shirdi,' he continued respectfully, 'Would you accompany us and grace the occasion with your presence?'

The *fakir* readily accepted the invitation and agreed to accompany Chand Patil and his family to Shirdi.

The Khandoba Temple where Baba first arrived in Shirdi

The Discovery

A few days later, Chand Patil's marriage party made its way to Shirdi. The bride was resplendent in her new clothes. She rode in a bullock cart that was decorated with bright flowers. She was accompanied by her mother and sisters, her face covered with a veil. She was feeling rather bashful at the prospect of meeting her husband-to-be, whom she had never seen before. As was the custom, her husband had been chosen by her family. Chand Patil and the rest of the family followed, some in bullock carts, others on foot, all dressed in their best clothes. They were accompanied by the customary musicians. The sound of drums and cymbals and bugles livened up the morning. The *fakir* walked along with them, not talking very much. He seemed immersed in his own thoughts. The group moved on, eager to reach Shirdi before noon. The sun was now beginning to make its presence felt and there was heat emanating from the dry, dusty roads.

At last they reached Shirdi. The village bore a festive look, for a wedding was an important occasion for everyone. All the villagers took part in the celebrations, which went on for many days. There would be feasting and entertainment and a chance to make merry.

On reaching Shirdi, the marriage party was received at the Khandoba temple on the outskirts of the village. Each member of Chand Patil's group was welcomed. Each one was addressed by his proper name and treated with great honour. It was soon the turn of the striking, young *fakir*. But nobody knew his name. How was he to be addressed? People looked at each other in embarrassment. After all, it would not do to insult any member of the marriage party.

It was then that the temple priest, Mhalsapati, stepped forward. It seemed obvious to him that this was no ordinary person. He stood out in the crowd, standing straight and tall. There was something about him that drew attention. 'Welcome Sai,' said Mhalsapati, using the term of respect for saintly persons. Everyone heaved a sigh of relief. That is how Sai Baba got his name.

That was also the first time that I set eyes upon Baba. I was a small girl then and never realized that this stranger would have such an impact on our lives. I stood there watching the welcoming ceremony, holding my little sister by the hand.

'Laxmitai, who is that man?' asked Rukma, my sister, rather loudly. The *fakir* turned around and smiled at us. The first thought that entered my mind was that he had the brightest pair of eyes I had ever seen! I could not look away from that powerful, piercing gaze!"

"Did Baba stay on in Shirdi after that?" asks Saraswati, almost nodding off to sleep.

"Saru, you should now go to bed. I will continue my story tomorrow."

"Please Aji, only a little more," they plead in unison.

"Alright, alright." I don't really need much persuasion. Recounting stories of Baba helps to ease my pain and I happily go on with my narration.

ONE OF US

Baba initially lived in the forest on the outskirts of Shirdi. We would see him when he came into the village to collect alms. A *kafni*-clad figure walking purposefully into the village; he spoke to no one. 'Allah Malik' was all he said when he received alms. Sometimes we would pass him in the narrow streets and run the other way. People called him the 'mad *fakir*'. He never interfered with anyone and was usually found spending long hours meditating under a Neem tree.

There was no doubt that he had achieved a very high level of spiritual powers. It was said that he performed some very difficult yogic exercises.

"Do you know, children, one day, my best friend Vithu came charging into my house, followed by our little group of friends.

'Laxmi, come quick, we've heard the most fantastic thing,' he panted.

I rushed out, eager to hear what juicy bit of news Vithu had brought.

'Well?' I asked impatiently.

'Do you know what the mad *fakir* did last night?' he

whispered conspiratorially. 'He took out his intestines, washed them and put them back,' he continued with round-eyed wonder.

'What nonsense you talk Vithu,' I said dismissively.

'It's true, Laxmi,' chorused the others. "Ramukaka saw it with his own eyes."

'Ramukaka saw it?' I asked, amazed. Ramukaka was one of our village elders and a very respected person. No one could doubt his word.

'Let's go and see what the mad *fakir* is doing now,' I said excitedly, and we all rushed to the Neem tree. Alas, nothing exciting was happening there. The mad *fakir* was only filling his *chillum*, all his body parts intact!"

"That is amazing, Aji," says Narsimha, awe in his voice.

"That's not all, Narsimha. We also heard other stories from time to time about his unbelievable yogic practice of taking out various organs from his body. Sometimes, they said, his arms and legs used to lie disjointed all over the place!"

"Really? Could he really sever his limbs from his body? Did you see that Aji?" asks a fascinated Kashinath.

"No, unfortunately not," I laugh. "We tried very hard but never succeeded."

"Aji, is it true that Baba slept on a narrow wooden plank

hanging high up from the ceiling?" asks Narsimha.

"Yes, that is true Narsimha. It was a wooden plank not more than six inches wide, fastened to the ceiling with rags at both ends. At the head and foot of the plank there would be oil lamps burning."

"But Aji, how did he climb on to it if it was suspended so high up?" asks Saru, stupefied.

"Nobody knows, Saru. No one ever saw him actually climb onto it or get off it. But people have seen him lying on it. It was one more of his *siddhis*, his yogic powers."

"That's truly something Aji," says Narsimha.

"Yes, all this sounded absolutely fantastic to us children. The mad *fakir* became a kind of local hero. One part of us was a little bit in awe of this strange man while another part wanted to find out more about these wonderful feats that he seemed to be able to accomplish. We would dare each other to run up to touch the Neem tree. Or to stop him in the street and talk to him. I think the closest we got to bravery though, was to hide behind some trees at a safe distance and peep at him. Although at that stage Baba was not a part of the village he had unconsciously started becoming a part of our lives.

Do you know what Dwarkamai used to be, children? It was a small, old *masjid*. It was in a dilapidated, broken down condition and nobody ever prayed there. It had been lying unused for years and years. We often used it as our playground. The uneven ground had big pits and stumbling

Shri Dwarkamai

holes, making it dangerously exciting to play there. The old, moss covered walls and crumbling pillars provided a perfect hiding place. But one day, to our consternation, we found that our private little nook had been taken over. After spending many years under the Neem tree, the 'mad *fakir*' had decided to come and live in the village. He had made the *masjid* his home! He named it 'Dwarkamai' or 'Mother Dwarka', the home of Lord Krishna."

"Were people nasty to him when he came to live in the village, Aji?" asks Saraswati.

"No, Saru, by this time, the local people had taken quite a liking to the *fakir*. The villagers had started calling him 'Baba'. Stories had spread about his ability to cure illnesses. The villagers would go to Baba to get medicines for their ailments and Baba would obligingly supply them with herbal medicines. Oh, he cured so many, many people of their incurable ailments. No one was ever turned away."

"That is wonderful, Aji," says Narsimha.

"Yes, he was always full of kindness, caring only for the well-being of others. He never really gave a thought to himself, giving generously of his time and love to all who came to him."

"So finally people accepted him as a holy man?" asks Saru.

"Yes, they did. For, you see, children, there was also something very special about him. His face and his demeanour suggested that he was no ordinary person.

Everyone in Shirdi had slowly come to accept him. Other holy men who passed through Shirdi held him in high regard and always treated him with the utmost respect.

As for us children, we finally had an opportunity to go near enough to find out what he was really like. When I came face to face with him once more after so many years, it was again his eyes that caught my attention – they were the brightest eyes I had ever seen, shining with some divine light."

"What did he say to you the first time you met him Aji?" asks Saraswati curiously.

"He didn't say much, Saru," I answer. No, he hadn't said much in words, he didn't really need to.

My mind takes me back in time to that wondrous day in Dwarkamai. I can still see him clearly, stirring the big cauldron he had placed on the fire. We waited for him to turn around. He saw us then, looking from my mother to me. There was a smile upon his gentle face. I held on tightly to my mother's hand, an overawed little girl hiding behind her mother's *sari pallav*. "I was about your age then, Saru, and in all honesty, I was a little frightened to be meeting the 'mad *fakir*'," I add, smiling at the memory.

"I bowed down before him at my mother's prodding and then, strangely, as I looked up at his face, all fear just vanished. 'Allah Malik' was all he said, raising his hand in blessing. But I felt as though I was surrounded by a sea of love and warmth. His beautiful eyes just exuded so much compassion and gentleness. That was it. From that day he was my friend and guide and Guru. He became someone very important in my life."

I stop to take a deep breath and take hold of my emotions before continuing.

"Life in Shirdi changed after Baba's arrival. All at once Baba became the focal point of the village. He used to visit certain houses to collect alms every morning. The *masjid*, which he had fondly named 'Dwarkamai', saw a daily stream of visitors. I used to go to Dwarkamai everyday, sometimes with the *bhakris* my mother had prepared for Baba, sometimes accompanying my father just for *darshan* or on other occasions, taking my siblings along to hear Baba tell his stories. He always welcomed us, giving us sweets or fruits. Those were happy, carefree times. We lived in our little village, unaware of what went on in the rest of the world.

There were, of course, those in our village who disliked Baba. But they were few and their attempts to influence the villagers failed miserably. I think they were rather jealous of Baba's popularity amongst the local people. Baba was loved and revered by us all. We had come to believe that he was unique and nothing could convince us otherwise."

There is the sound of a bullock cart in the street outside. It is my neighbour Ganesh, the children's father. They run to meet him. He has been at Dwarkamai since afternoon and he looks tired. Baba was an important part of his life too and I can see that he acutely feels the pain of parting from Baba.

"What happened at Dwarkamai?" I ask.

He shakes his head with a sad look. "There is a debate about what rites to perform – Hindu or Muslim," answers Ganesh.

"But Baba had expressed his wish to be buried in Buti's Wada, so why should there be a problem?" I persist.

"It is difficult to get everybody to agree," sighs Ganesh. "But I'm sure it will be resolved soon."

"I hope so," I answer, feeling a sense of despondency overtake me. A dispute like this went against the very core of Baba's teachings.

"Nothing will ever be the same again," I think to myself. "Just like nothing was the same after Baba arrived in Shirdi."

CONSTRUCTION OF BUTI'S WADA

It is almost two weeks since Baba attained *nirvana*. The controversy about his resting place was quickly resolved and he was interred in Buti's Wada. An edifice was also raised over his grave. This is now Baba's final resting place. I feel happy that he has been buried here. That had been his wish and it is right that his wish has been respected.

I have come to Buti's Wada today to pay my respects to Baba just as I have done almost every day in the past two weeks. Sitting here in silence, chanting the *Sai-japa* brings me immense peace. I am happy that this *wada* was constructed by Buti. The events leading to its construction were strange, to say the least.

Buti was a devotee of Baba. One night he had a dream. In his dream Baba asked him to build a *wada*, a big house, with a temple. Strangely enough, the same night, another devotee, Madhavrao Deshpande, fondly called Shama by Baba, also had the same dream. The next day, amazed at having had the same dream, they decided to draw up the plans for a *wada*. Buti, being a wealthy man, agreed to fund the construction. The plans were thereafter blessed by Baba and construction commenced. The construction activity took place at a furious pace and the *wada* started taking shape. Baba took keen interest in the construction of the *wada*.

Baba's Samadhi

Sometimes while passing by the construction site, Baba would stop and look in, even making his own suggestions.

On the ground floor of the *wada* there was to be a temple. Buti was very keen that an idol of Murlidhar – the flute-playing Krishna – be installed there. One day, when Baba happened to come into the *wada*, he was told of Buti's wish. "Of course," said Baba, "and when the temple is built, we shall also inhabit it and live ever after in joy!"

Buti was very content. "Baba has promised to live in the *wada*," he thought happily.

An order for a statue of Murlidhar was placed and construction continued rapidly.

However it was at this time that Baba fell ill and it seemed to all that he would not live to see the *wada* or the temple in it. "Why did Baba appear in my dream and instruct me to build this *wada* if he will never live in it?" thought Buti miserably.

And then Baba's condition worsened. The end seemed inevitable. In his last moments, Baba asked to be moved to Buti's Wada. "I will be happier there," he told the devotees. This was one of the last things he said. At 2.35 p.m. Baba became one with the Eternal Power.

It was then that the unfortunate debate over his body started. Had people learned nothing from Baba after all these years? But finally, his desire to be interred in the *wada* was accepted by all concerned. So Baba did come to live in Buti's Wada. He had obviously meant to live there in his own way. He

The Original Samadhi Mandir

A later photograph of the Samadhi Mandir

had decided to make it his final resting place. The day after he gave up his physical body, Baba's body was interred in the *wada*. This place is now the Samadhi Mandir for all of Baba's numerous devotees, a place to commune with him and seek solace and comfort.

Sitting here I can feel his presence. Saints like Baba live on even after giving up the physical body. Their spirit continues to exist, creating powerful vibrations all around. One can feel the tremendous charged energy in the atmosphere. And if one truly wants to communicate with him, he is there. His spirit lives on, filling our life with his love and compassion. He is there for all to see if only one has the vision to see him. He is there for all to have if only one has the inclination to ask for him. He is there for all to love if only one has the good fortune to love and be loved by him.

LIGHTS BURNED WITHOUT OIL

Dusk is fast approaching and the three children are lighting *puntees*, the little clay pots filled with oil. I have been invited by my neighbours, for today is Laxmipooja, an important day during Diwali. Diwali, the festival of lights, celebrates the homecoming of Lord Rama after fourteen years of exile. It is said that to welcome him home the entire city of *Ayodhya* had been decorated with little *puntees,* denoting the triumph of light over darkness. Looking at their happy faces, I am glad that we have decided to celebrate Diwali at least in a small way. It is three weeks since Dassera and there is no enthusiasm to celebrate amongst the adults. But it seemed unfair to deprive the children of their fun and to dampen their spirits. Moreover, Baba would not have liked to see the little ones unhappy. He was always so fond of children, believing them to be innocent and god-like. So the decision was taken – *puntees* to be lit, special Diwali food to be prepared, and new clothes to be made for the children.

Narsimha and Saraswati are on vacation. Kashinath is still too young to go to school. We have one Marathi school in Shirdi, which the children attend. It offers education up to the seventh class. Higher education is possible only in Ahmednagar, which is a fair distance from here. Consequently, instead of schooling further, many children take to the family profession.

Lights Burned Without Oil

"Can we try lighting the lamps with water instead of oil?" asks Narsimha, tongue-in-cheek. His reference to the time Baba had no oil to light lamps makes me laugh.

"No one can light lamps with water, silly," shoots back Saru, quite sure she has got the better of her older brother for once.

"You can, if you are Baba," answers Narsimha smugly. "Isn't that right, Aji?"

"Did Baba do that?" asks Saru, her large black eyes full of wonder. "You have never told me this story, Aji," she adds accusingly. "Tell me, please."

"Wait for me, I'm coming too," squeals Kashinath, rushing off to put down his *puntee*.

"Alright, there is still some time for the *pooja*," I reply. "Come and sit down."

Once they settle themselves down comfortably, I begin.

"Every evening, as the sun set over Shirdi and little lamps cast a dull glow in every house, Baba used to light *puntees* in Dwarkamai. Of course, as Saru rightly pointed out, these lamps need oil. But Baba being a *fakir* had no money to buy oil. So the grocers of Shirdi would give him oil free of charge. This went on for many years and the lamps burned every evening in the *masjid*. Devotees would gather there in the evenings to see Baba. I remember the numerous evenings I accompanied my parents to Dwarkamai. We children used

Baba setting out to collect alms

to run around, playing games and drifting in and out of the gathering. Often, Baba would call us to sit beside him and tell us stories. He was very fond of the children of Shirdi and the children in turn were totally devoted to him. By the light of the oil-lamps Baba conducted many a discussion with the devotees. I was too young to understand all that was talked about but the adults sat there in rapt attention, listening to his every word.

Now, the grocers of Shirdi had become greedy and did not want to supply the oil free anymore.

'Why should we give him oil everyday?' grumbled Premchand.

'He never pays us anything,' added Gopichand.

'Let us refuse to give him the oil the next time he comes around,' said Premchand.

Next day, as usual, Baba came to the grocers to collect his oil.

'Some oil please,' he said, smiling, as he held out his mug at Premchand's shop.

The grocer had been poring over his books, his thick, bushy eyebrows almost covering his eyes. He was a large, fat man, dressed in a *dhoti* and shirt. A white turban sat on his head at a peculiar angle. On hearing Baba's voice he looked up.

'I don't have any oil today Baba,' he lied silkily.

Baba's face briefly reflected his surprise. Without a word of protest he went on to the second grocer. Gopichand was waiting for him. He looked at Baba with sharp, narrow eyes, ready with his words of denial.

Before Baba could hold out his mug he shiftily said, 'Premchand told you, there is no oil today.'

'No oil today!' repeated Baba, looking piercingly at the grocer.

Gopichand could not look Baba in the eye and quickly turned away, a guilty look on his face.

Baba did not get angry. 'Allah Malik,' he said and quietly made his way back to Dwarkamai.

That evening, unaware of what had transpired, I went to Dwarkamai with my father and sisters. There was already a gathering of people, eager to ask Baba for advice or just to seek his blessings. I seated myself next to Baba. He gave me a warm smile and patted my head. More and more people started arriving. As the last rays of the sun slowly disappeared, Baba started arranging the little clay pots as usual. I jumped up, eager to light the lamps. It was one of my childish pleasures, helping him fill the pots with oil and placing them all over Dwarkamai.

'Where is the oil, Baba?' I inquired innocently, finding that the mug was empty.

'There is no oil today, Laxmi,' he murmured, a sad look on his face.

Lights Burned Without Oil

'Then how are we to light the lamps?' I asked, crestfallen.

'Do not worry, child,' he said. 'There shall be light.'

So saying, he took the mug from me. At the bottom of the mug were a few drops of leftover oil. Baba added water to it and saying a prayer, proceeded to drink it all. He then filled the mug with fresh water and handed it to me, saying, 'Here, fill the pots with this water.'

The people gathered around were surprised. What was Baba talking about? 'How will the lamps burn without oil?' they thought to themselves. But somehow no such doubts arose in my trusting young mind. I promptly proceeded to fill the pots with water and watched eagerly as Baba lit them.

And wonder of wonders, the lights not only burned but they lasted well into the night, for many, many hours."

"You actually saw this happen, Aji?" asks Saru, awestruck.

"Yes," I answer wistfully. "Baba's powers were unique."

"But Aji, what happened to the grocers? Did Baba punish them?" questions Kashinath, quite aghast that anyone could refuse Baba anything.

"No Kashi, this was punishment enough for them. Of course the next day they heard about Baba's miracle. They felt very ashamed. They came at once to Baba.

'Why didn't you truthfully tell me that you did not want to

give me the oil?' he asked the grocers. 'It is very wrong to tell a lie.'

The grocers begged him to forgive them, which he willingly did. They realized that here was a true Spiritual Master. But instead of comprehending his greatness, they had shown their own weakness of mind and spirit. Shame-faced, they asked Baba for spiritual guidance.

'Oh Master, you are the embodiment of the realised self. Show us the way.'

Baba was kindness personified. He looked at the grocers for a moment and spoke in his calm voice. 'Greed knows no peace, nor contentment, nor freedom from care. Once greed is entrenched in the mind it ruins all spiritual progress. It leaves no scope for concentration or meditation. How then can you find the way?'

'What should we do to free ourselves, Maharaj?' asked the grocers, feeling mortified.

'He, whose mind is engrossed with accumulation of wealth, will not find *jnana* unless the impediment of wealth is removed. The temptation of wealth is difficult to overcome. It is like crossing a deep, dark river infested with crocodiles. Only he who is free from desire will survive. Therefore, give up this desire for worldly things and purify your mind. Then you will see for yourself the path to spiritual progress.' "

I remember how these words did not seem to make much sense to me at that tender age. But now, when I go over those same simple words, they hold a wealth of meaning.

Suddenly Kashinath jumps up excitedly. "Look Aji, there's Laxmi." We all turn to look. There is a little frog hopping near the kitchen door. It is believed that a frog coming into the house on Laxmipooja day is actually Laxmi, the Goddess of Wealth. Doors to every house are kept wide open on this day to make sure that Laxmi hops into the house and blesses its inhabitants with lots of wealth in the coming year. So our little amphibian visitor is an honoured guest indeed! The children hover around the frog excitedly, willing it to take one last big jump into the house.

Soon there is a loud cheer from the children. Laxmi has finally thought it fit to enter the house to the accompaniment of loud clapping. I watch the delight on the faces of the children. Some day they will learn to appreciate real wealth – the wealth of Baba's teachings.

"It's time for the *pooja*," announces Janki from inside the house. She has now got everything organized in her quiet, efficient way. We go into the house enthusiastically.

Half an hour later we are standing before the small temple at one end of the kitchen. This is our first Diwali without Baba but he is present in all our hearts. I continue singing the *arati* joyously, reminiscing about all the previous times I have sung the *arati* in Baba's presence.

AND THE WELL OVERFLOWED...

Spring has arrived earlier than usual this year. The *jowar* crop is flourishing in the fields and will soon need to be harvested. The fields look beautiful in the early morning light, like a sea of gently undulating golden-yellow waves. The tips of the *jowar* plants sway lightly in the breeze, the morning dew glistening on the leaves. There is a fresh, crisp feel in the air. All around there are sounds of cowbells and bullock carts. Turbaned farmers bustle about, greeting each other, ready to start work in the fields. This is a busy time of the year for the villagers. Most of them own some plots of land and cultivate crops. They normally keep half of what they harvest for their own needs and sell the balance in the market. *Jowar, bajri,* wheat, maize and sugarcane are the main crops cultivated in this area. Ganesh will be working long hours in the fields with help from Janki and the children.

The children are in the courtyard, playing with some shiny round stones they found near the well yesterday. It is time for Narsimha and Saraswati to leave for school but they are engrossed in their game. The glasses of milk and some *bhakris* that their mother has kept ready for them are forgotten.

"Children, hurry up, drink up your milk," I call.

"Aji, my friend Dattu says that the fair is to be held soon,"

Saru states between mouthfuls of *bhakri*. "Will they enact the Ramayana again this year?"

"I think they will; after all, the fair is held on Rama Navami day. Did you enjoy it last year?"

"Very much," says Narsimha, giggling. "Specially the part where Sita's hair fell off."

"Narsimha!" I admonish, unable to suppress a smile. You see, women do not take part in these plays, and all the roles are enacted by men. Last year, the boy portraying Sita was very uncomfortable with the wig he was wearing. And to the lad's great embarrassment, at the climax of Sita's *swayamvara*, the wig fell off. It was quite hilarious. I suspect that the thunderous applause he received at the end was more for the amusement generated than for any thespian skills!

"You know children, in the first year of the fair we almost cancelled it. It was thanks to Baba that the fair took place."

"How so, Aji?" Kashinath's curiosity is aroused.

"Well, it is one more of Baba's *leelas*. Your father was a wee lad then. I remember how excited he was. It had been decided to organize a fair to celebrate the festival of Rama Navami. Baba's blessings were sought and plans were made. Our sleepy old village was soon to be the centre of festivity.

Everyone was naturally excited. Everyone wanted to make the celebrations a grand success. After all, it was not every day that one organized a fair in the village.

Rama Navami celebrations in Shirdi

But our excitement was short-lived. That evening, Khandukaka, our village headman, summoned everyone to the village square for a meeting. 'Friends,' he said, 'We have a problem. As you all know, we have only one well in our village and it has almost dried up. We simply cannot organize a fair without good water supply. We are sure to have a lot of visitors. We will need water to drink, cook, bathe and wash. Our water reserves just won't suffice. I am afraid we will have to cancel the fair.' Nobody said a word as the meaning of what Khandukaka was saying sank in. Suddenly all the gaiety vanished and gloom took its place. Everyone realized the truth of the old man's words."

"Was the water shortage worse than usual, Aji?" asks Narsimha seriously.

"Yes, Narsimha," I answer, looking at his intent little face. Working with his father in the fields, little Narsimha has begun to understand the difficulties of his elders. It is a pity that he has to grow up so fast. But reality is a harsh teacher. We have always had a water problem in our part of the world. In this vast district of Ahmednagar in Maharashtra, we are no strangers to drought. We live in a land of scanty rainfall and an arid climate. The news of the wells almost drying up was therefore not totally unexpected. I think in our eagerness to hold the fair we had willed ourselves to forget our problem.

"All the children were most disappointed. Your father was almost in tears. A great discussion followed but no decision could be reached. What were we to do?

'Let us go to Baba and ask his advice,' said someone finally.

Rama Navami celebrations in Shirdi

'He will surely know what is to be done.' Baba had become a source of strength for everyone.

So Khandukaka and some other elders went to Dwarkamai.

'Is that all?' Baba asked, amused, when he had heard them out. 'We shall overcome this problem.' So saying, he gave Khandukaka some leaves with *prasad* on them.

'Drop these into our village well and you shall have more water than you can use,' said Baba calmly.

With great enthusiasm they at once did as they were bid. And then...."

"Then what, Aji? Do tell," says Saru, anticipation writ large on her face.

"And then, before our astonished eyes the well started filling up as though by magic. It filled and filled and filled.... until it almost overflowed."

"That is so awesome," exclaims Saru.

"So from that time the fair has been taking place every year," says Narsimha. He pauses to think for a moment. "Aji, how did Baba become such a great man? Did he have a Guru?" he asks wonderingly.

"Well Narsimha, though there are many stories about Baba's Guru, nobody knows for certain who he was."

"Aren't you children going to school today?" shouts their mother from inside the house.

"Going Aai," they yell, picking up their schoolbags and rushing out. "Bye Aji, remember, you have to continue your story later."

WHO WAS BABA'S GURU?

We are standing under the Neem tree, the children and I. Keeping my promise of telling them the story of Baba's Guru, I decide to bring them here. All afternoon, they have been working, stacking bundles of grass in one corner of the field. This grass will be used to feed the cattle. With water being as scarce as it is, we have to stock up as much grass as we can.

They have all, of course, been here before. But today I want them to experience the atmosphere here, to feel the vibrations around us as I talk of Baba's years of penance. It is not easy to explain to such young minds all the philosophy surrounding Baba's life and teachings.

"Why have we come here, Aji?" inquires Kashinath, looking around him.

"You wanted to know about Baba's Guru, didn't you? Well..."

I hold Kashi by the shoulders and turn him around.

"There," I point at a spot under the Neem tree, "is an underground cell where it is said, Baba practiced meditation for 12 years. Some say that he spent these years in the company of his Guru, others say he was alone. No one knows

Gurusthan under the Neem tree

for sure but he certainly spent those years in penance."

"Can we go in there? Is it a dark, mysterious cave?" Saru's eyes are dancing with eagerness.

"No, Saru," I answer, "it has been sealed. Nobody can go in there anymore."

"Did Baba ever mention his Guru?" asks Narsimha.

"Well, he made many references to his Guru or *aulia* but never disclosed who he really was. He did mention to people that he had spent twelve years in his company. 'My Guru was both a mother and father to me. He gave me all the spiritual guidance that I needed,' Baba used to say."

"How was this cell discovered, Aji?" asks Saraswati, curiously.

"That, Saru, is an absolutely amazing tale. One day, at the Khandoba fair, someone went into a trance…" My memory is jogged and I go back in time to one of the most awesome days of my life. It is quite a common occurrence at these fairs. It is said that spirits take over a person's body and can answer any questions. People ask all sorts of questions to these spirits.

"The Khandoba fair was an annual occurrence and it was a day we all looked forward to as children. That day, along with the other children of the village, I had excitedly taken part in all the proceedings. We played games and indulged our palates with those special sweets that seemed to be prepared only on that occasion. My favourite haunt at the fair though was the bangle stall. I used to gaze in fascination at the myriad glass bangles neatly arranged over paper tubes. Hues of red and green and purple in all sizes. As a special treat every year I would be given my choice of bangles by my father. I had just picked out a bright orange pair when I heard the commotion. Shouts of 'Hurry, she has gone into a trance' filled the air. Everyone rushed to the temple without further thought. My orange bangles were forgotten for the moment.

Making my way to the front of the crowd, I witnessed a fearful sight. I was shocked into immobility. I saw a woman standing before the deity, her long black hair loose, a coin-sized red *kumkum* on her forehead. To me, she seemed possessed by some streak of insanity as she swayed madly round and round, her long hair flying in all directions about her face, her dazed eyes staring upwards. She uttered strange cries from time to time and lunged backward and forward. I was rooted to the spot, watching the scene in a kind of fascinated horror. I had never before encountered such a sight.

Someone then asked the spirit to reveal who Baba's Guru was. There was dead silence in the crowd as everyone waited expectantly for some revelation. The woman continued swaying and muttering in her trance and then spoke in a strange, deep voice. 'Dig up the spot under the Neem tree and you will find out.'

The indicated spot was, of course, promptly dug up and a most fascinating sight greeted us. Our eyes beheld a cellar with a *paat*, a kind of low stool and four lighted lamps. It was unbelievable! Then the spirit said, 'This is the place where Baba spent 12 years in meditation.'

Who Was Baba's Guru?

When Baba was asked about it he quietly replied, 'That is the place of my Guru,' but he refrained from naming him."

"Does that mean that Baba always lived in Shirdi? Didn't you tell us that he came here with Chandbhai?" asks a puzzled Narsimha.

"Well, the story of Baba's birth remains shrouded in mystery. But it is believed that he was born in a Hindu Brahmin family and that when he was eight years old he was taken away by a Sufi *fakir*. Sufi *fakirs* are holy men of the Muslim faith. He spent many years in his Guru's company and during this time he probably lived in this underground cell. He then must have spent some years as a wandering *fakir* before coming to Shirdi with Chandbhai."

"Why does one have to meditate and go through all this penance to become like Baba?" asks Narsimha. "What does one have to achieve?"

I pause to reflect on his question. Narsimha has asked a highly philosophical question which has no simple answer. It is not easy to explain philosophy to a child, far less easy for him to understand it.

"Alright," I say, "let me try to explain it to you the way Baba explained it to me. You all know what a chariot is, don't you?"

There are nods all around. "Yes, it's a carriage drawn by horses," answers Kashi, knowledgeably.

"That's right. And who drives the chariot?" I ask.

"The charioteer, of course," comes Saru's prompt response.

"Well, tell me, what would happen if the charioteer did not know how to drive?" I ask, looking at the three, by now puzzled, faces.

"The horses would run helter-skelter, there would be chaos," answers Narsimha.

"Exactly. Now think of your body as the chariot. Let your intellect or what we call *buddhi*, be the charioteer and then you, the *jeevatma* or the soul, sit in the chariot as the master, with a mind calm and composed. The master has to tell the charioteer where he wants to go and guide him along. The charioteer in turn has to control his horses, who are like our sense organs, wild and impetuous. So, as long as the master guides the horses through the charioteer, he is fine. But if the horses are allowed to have their way, there would be, as Narsimha rightly pointed out, chaos."

"Do you understand?" I ask, looking around at their intent little faces.

"Yes, Aji," says Narsimha. "That is why spiritual persons like Baba meditate and search for the true path. They can thereby completely control their mind and intellect."

"That's very good, Narsimha," I say, admiringly. "When we go on a journey we have to know the road, right? In the same way, when we undertake the journey of life, we have to know the right road to take or else we get lost. And once we get lost, we go around in circles trying to find our way again.

Some of us never do. Therefore it is very important to have a Guru who can guide us."

"That is easy to understand Aji," says Narsimha. "Did Baba always explain everything so simply?"

"Yes, he did," I remember fondly. There were of course those numerous occasions when Baba talked in a highly intellectual manner. But he always made sure he conveyed his message depending upon the person he was addressing.

"Aji, we are lucky that Baba chose to make Shirdi his home, aren't we?" says Narsimha.

"Yes child, we are blessed indeed," I agree wholeheartedly.

SUFI SYNTHESIS

"Aji, you told us that Baba's Guru was a Sufi. What does that mean? Who are Sufis?" asks Saru. Are they different from *Sanyasis*?"

"Well, yes and no, Saru. Externally they are different, in their dress, language and even the path to God. But beyond a certain point, all differences melt away because one comes closer to the Divine."

"How do you mean?" Kashi is puzzled.

"It is simple, Kashi," chimes in Narsimha. "There are different roads leading to the village school, aren't there? We could take any route we liked, different routes, but there would be a point where we all would meet as we approached the school. Isn't that right, Aji?"

"Yes, absolutely, and would it really matter, at that point, which road you had walked on?" I say.

"Hmm," says Saru, "but what exactly is Sufism?"

"Sufism can be described as Islamic mysticism. A Sufi is actually one who has attained God-realization. He is one who has reached a stage where he has experienced a spiritual union with God. He has given up a worldly life in search of the

Infinite. But the term, as it is generally used, means a Muslim mystic, even one who is still in search of the Eternal," I reply.

"So, a Sufi is the equivalent of a *sanyasi*?" asks Saru.

"That's right. A Sufi is sometimes also called a *fakir*, and is like a Muslim *sanyasi* or yogi."

"Aji, where did Sufism originate?" asks Narsimha curiously.

"Well, Sufism has its origin in the Koran, the holy book of the Muslims. You know that the Koran is the word of God, revealed to the Prophet Mohammad. Sufism is the mystical element of the Prophet's teaching. It is based on experience, on spiritual insight. Sufism has taken root in our part of the world but it evolved in Persia and Arabia, about a century or two after the death of Prophet Mohammad. It then started spreading and a few hundred years ago, many Sufi divines arrived in India. Individual Sufi Masters then set up their own orders of Sufism."

"How many orders are there?" asks Kashi.

"In India, we have four orders, Kashi – Chishtia, Qadirriya, Suhwardiya and Nakshbandi, but they all essentially have the same goal, that of God-realization."

"Aji, if Sufis are Islamic mystics, how is Sufism different from Islam?" questions Saru.

"Some of the aspects of Sufism are not in conformity with mainstream Islam. Therefore, Sufism has not always been completely accepted within the fold of Islam," I answer.

"In what way?" Saru probes.

"Well, Sufis do not accept the ritualistic practices of orthodox Islam. This sometimes leads to conflict with the mainstream religion. Let me tell you a little about the tenets of Sufism. That will help you understand something about Sufism. Baba had imbibed Sufi teachings and thought through his Guru.

Sufis believe that there is one God and that to attain a level of spiritual unity with God, one must give up a material existence. Since it is rooted in mysticism, Sufism stresses the importance of direct experience. It rejects rituals and rites. Baba, too, always emphasized the need for devotion to God as against mere bookish knowledge. He was forever repeating the Lord's name, pronouncing it to be the most powerful means of reaching Him. And like many other streams of religious thought, Sufism speaks of the pivotal role of the *Murshid* or Guru, without whom, one finds it very hard to reach one's spiritual destination."

Narsimha looks thoughtful. "Aji," he says at length, "all this sounds so much like the teachings of the Hindu Bhakti saints."

"True," I smile. "Children, the core of mysticism, wherever it stems from, is the same but it gets coloured by the prevailing religious, political and cultural situation of the region. There is a lot of similarity between Sufis and the Bhakti saints of India. Both streams are based on love for God, believing in total surrender to Him and the Guru. Mystics from both religions give utmost importance to a direct experience of God and therefore do not conform to the orthodox religion and its incumbent ritualistic practices. Baba too believed in showing the way to God-realization without following any formal religion. He called himself neither Hindu nor Muslim, knowing that the ultimate goal for any seeker was the same. He therefore encouraged his disciples to seek God through the medium of their own religion. And that is why he was totally against conversion. I remember, once, when a Hindu convert to Islam came to him, Baba got very angry and slapped him, saying, 'Aren't you ashamed to change your father?'. He always tried to explain to his disciples that external factors do not really count on the spiritual journey, what is needed is a love of God, a passionate desire to seek Him and find ultimate bliss in the mystical union with Him."

"Baba's attitude must have surely upset many people," comments Saru.

"Oh, yes. Baba was often confronted by local Muslims because of his non-conformist manner. They wanted him to follow Muslim rituals like the Friday prayers, which he refused to do. Some of them threatened to kill the Hindus who, they felt, were corrupting Baba, and, in fact, one of them was ready to kill Baba himself."

There are horrified gasps from the children.

"Of course, Baba's detractors were impotent in the face of his spiritual powers and could harm no one," I hasten to tell them.

"Aji, Baba's teachings, then, are a blend of Sufism and Hinduism," Narsimha ponders aloud.

"Yes, a beautiful synthesis, Narsimha," I concur. "Baba's teachings are a synchronized blend of Sufism and Bhakti. It is believed that Baba was born a Hindu but his Guru was a Sufi. Baba always taught that the best way to God was through *Naam*, constant chanting of the Lord's name. He stressed the importance of a Guru to guide one through the quagmire of this illusory life; to always keep the Guru in mind and meditate upon him. You see, children, the openness of Sufism and the Bhakti movement had already created a lot of interaction between the two communities. Hindus and Muslims both visited the tombs of Sufi Masters. Baba encouraged this confluence in his own way, by combining the celebration of the Hindu Rama Navami with the Muslim *Urs*, thus fostering religious harmony and brotherhood. His lived his life, until the very end, in pursuit of unity amongst all religions. Do you know, when he divined that the end was drawing near, about four months before giving up the ghost, he sent some people from Shirdi to Aurangabad to meet a Sufi mystic, Hazrat Shamsuddin Baba. He sent him Rs. 250 to perform some rituals as per Sufi tradition. These included *maulu* (singing praises of the Prophet), *qawwali* (singing praises of auliyas) and *nyas* (distribution of food). And then, two weeks before his Samadhi, Baba listened as one of his Hindu disciples read aloud the *Ramavijaya* to him."

"Baba can be claimed by both traditions, Sufism and Bhakti," says Narsimha softly, "but then, on the other hand, he belonged to neither…..he was just Baba, a Perfect Master."

Narsimha has voiced my own thoughts. I am overcome with emotion on hearing his words. Baba had inherited the mantle of mysticism from Sufism as well as Bhakti. He knew the

Vedas, Upanishads, Bhagavad Gita as well as the Koran, Hadith and Masnavi. He was therefore able to transcend boundaries and touch the hearts of all, whether Hindu or Muslim. As Narsimha beautifully expressed it, Baba was both, and yet he was neither. He was a Perfect Master.

THE VANISHING TONGAWALLAH

It is almost dawn. The early morning is warm and humid, typical of a Shirdi summer. I wind my way to the back of the house, adjacent to the cowshed. There is a cluster of banana trees, hiding from view two large stone slabs which make up a small bathing area. I find two buckets filled with water. Everyday, Janki and the children bring me water in large earthen pots from the well. Some of it is used for bathing, some for cooking. The only other source of water is a small stream on the outskirts of the village. That is where a lot of the villagers bathe and wash clothes. I pray that the rainfall this year is good. Everything depends on the rain. But for whatever reason, the rain gods do not cast a favourable eye on us.

The cool water feels refreshing on the skin in this heat. By the time I finish, I can see the sun rising in the eastern sky. I bow down and make my salutations to the Sun God. Somewhere in the distance a rooster crows once. There is a gentle chirping of birds, which gets louder as they get ready to swoop down on unsuspecting prey. The rooster crows again and yet again like a loud, raucous alarm. I go into the kitchen to start my morning *pooja*.

I sit before the idols of Ganesh, Laxmi and Krishna. I bathe them and anoint them with fresh *haldi* and *kumkum*, all the while reciting *shlokas*. Taking my *japa-mala* and little box filled with *udi* I go out into the courtyard. *Udi* is the ash that is collected from the large *dhuni* or fire that Baba kept burning constantly in Dwarkamai.

The *dhuni* still burns in that same spot where it had been first lit by Baba and the ash is distributed to devotees. The *udi* has amazing powers of healing and Baba would often give it to people to cure illnesses. It is said to have the power to keep harm and misfortune away. I wistfully remember the numerous times Baba has applied *udi* on my forehead. The times that he gave us *udi* to cure some malaise or the other. I often used to ask Baba what wonderful power the *udi* had. "The power of faith," he used to reply, his radiant face emanating some powerful force.

There are so many touching stories of the faith of his devotees in the *udi* that Baba gave them. There is one particular incident that makes me emotional even today. I have heard this story told by Nanasaheb Chandorkar himself. I remember Nana's voice cracking with emotion when he narrated this story to us.

Nana's daughter Minatai was pregnant and as is the custom, had gone to her parents' house in Jamner for the birth of the child. The time for her delivery was fast approaching and the girl was going through a lot of trouble. With limited medical facilities, a difficult child-birth could be life threatening. The poor girl was in agony and nothing seemed to help to ease her pain. Nana and his wife were mighty worried. Nana, a staunch devotee of Baba, started praying to Baba and appealing for help. "Please Baba," he prayed, "Come to our aid."

The original Dhuni in Dwarkamai

The Vanishing Tongawallah

At that very same time Gosavi Ramgir, another of Baba's devotees, was in Shirdi. That morning, Ramgirbua, as he was called, had a sudden urge to visit his hometown in Khandesh. As was the custom in the village, he at once went to Baba to ask permission to leave. To his consternation, Baba said, "Of course you may go, but first go to Jamner and meet Nana. Find out if all is well with him and give him this packet of *udi*." So saying, he gave Ramgirbua some *udi* tied in a packet. Ramgirbua was puzzled. Jamner was not exactly en route to Khandesh. Moreover he only had two rupees in his pocket. How was he to travel to Jamner and to Khandesh with such little money? When he mentioned this to Baba, he replied, "Do not worry. You will be looked after." As far as Ramgirbua was concerned, that was assurance enough. He had known Baba long enough to know that even the most unfathomable requests had some deeper meaning. Without any further questioning, he made arrangements to leave Shirdi.

Getting to Jamner is not an easy task. There is no direct train to Jamner. The nearest railway station is Jalgaon from where one has to walk. Poor Ramgirbua! Getting off late at night at Jalgaon station, he was a worried man indeed. He had spent most of his two rupees on a ticket to Jalgaon. What was he to do now? As he came out of the station at about 3.00 a.m., considering the options before him, a welcome sight greeted his eyes. Standing at the gate was a tall man sporting a moustache and beard, asking the passengers as they came out, "Who is Ramgirbua of Shirdi?"

Ramgirbua stepped forward eagerly. "I am Ramgirbua," he said, addressing the tall stranger.

A pair of very dark eyes in a tanned face appraised Ramgirbua. "Nanasaheb has sent me with a *tonga* for you," said the man. "He is awaiting you."

Ramgirbua was ecstatic. Nanasaheb must have received a message from Shirdi, he thought. He got into the comfortable *tonga* and they set off for Jamner. They travelled the next few hours without stopping. At dawn, the *tongawallah* stopped near a stream to give the horses a rest. "Nanasaheb has sent something for you to eat," he told Ramgirbua, taking out some mangoes and *pedhas*. After they had both eaten and the horses had been given water, they set off again.

At sunrise they finally reached Jamner. The tonga made its way to Nanasaheb's house. Nanasaheb was extremely happy to see his friend Ramgirbua. He welcomed him into his house and enquired after him. Ramgirbua handed over the packet of *udi* to Nana and narrated Baba's strange request to visit him. Reaching for the packet of *udi*, Nanasaheb's face was a study in amazement. He explained to Ramgirbua the problem his daughter was facing and how he had appealed to Baba for help. The *udi* was at once mixed with water and given to the girl. As she drank it, the pain instantly stopped. And within minutes she delivered a healthy baby without any trouble. There was great jubilation in Nana's house.

Later, sitting in the *verandah* sipping hot tea, Ramgirbua said, "Nana, I must thank you for sending your *tonga* for me. I don't know what I would have done without it."

"*Tonga?*" asked Nana, puzzled. "What *tonga?* I never sent any *tonga* for you. Why, I didn't even know you were coming.

"But, but..." stammered a horrified Ramgirbua. "The *tongawallah* told me you had sent him. He should still be here."

They both at once rushed out to find the mysterious *tongawallah*. But there was no one in sight.

"Are you sure you came in a *tonga*?" Nana asked, looking doubtfully at Ramgirbua.

"Of course I did," said Ramgirbua indignantly. He looked around him, perplexed. "What could have become of him?"

They looked all over but they never did find the *tongawallah*. He seemed to have vanished into thin air. Funnily enough, nobody in the village seemed to have seen a *tonga* or *tongawallah* that morning. With so many people about, it would be impossible to miss a *tonga*! So where was it? And who was the *tongawallah*? As realization dawned, Ramgirbua narrated the whole story to Nana in great detail. Baba had come to his devotee's rescue, he had answered Nana's appeal for help. Both men were absolutely amazed.

Nana thereafter came to Shirdi to see Baba. He prostrated himself before Baba, too overwhelmed to speak. Later, he told us the wonderful tale of the mysterious *tongawallah*. As the story unfolded, there was not one amongst us who was not choked with emotion.

Although Baba's physical body was in Shirdi, he could take any form, anywhere. "This time it was a *tongawallah*, I wonder what it will be next time. Baba's powers are truly great," said Nana, tears of happiness streaming from his eyes.

Yes indeed, marvellous are the ways of the true Masters!

Sitting cross-legged on the *khaat,* I mentally repeat Baba's name. Everything around me is still and I immerse myself in Baba's name. I am lost to the world, lost in thoughts of Baba.

BABA'S INVISIBLE HAND

"Aji, Shantamaushi has come to Shirdi," says Saraswati, one afternoon, as we sit shelling peas. Of course, a large portion of the shelled peas find their way into her mouth.

"Shanta? Shanta Kirwandikar?" I repeat, pleasantly surprised.

Shanta is my childhood friend. We have spent many happy hours playing together as children. After her marriage, Shanta moved to her husband's hometown, a few hours away from Shirdi. She occasionally came to visit Baba with her family. Baba had been very fond of her and her relationship with him was very special. Baba had once miraculously saved her life.

"She said she would be visiting you today," says Saraswati.

Sometime later Shanta comes into the house. Apart from some greying of the hair she has changed little. She is still the same skinny girl I remember. We are always happy to see each other, Shanta and I. It is wonderful to meet old friends, to talk about old times and reflect on the course our lives have taken.

We spend a long time inquiring after each other and talking about common friends. We are somehow trying to avoid talking about Baba. This is Shanta's first visit after Baba's *samadhi* and it is painful for both of us to talk of him in the past. Finally, I tackle the subject.

"Did you visit the Samadhi Mandir?" I ask Shanta.

"Yes. I went there first, as soon as I arrived in Shirdi. It is so peaceful," she says. "But it feels very strange to be in Shirdi and not see Baba."

"Yes," I agree.

"But Laxmi," she adds slowly, "I know that he is still here amongst us. I feel it. He doesn't need a physical body to be present. I should know that better than anybody. Do you remember how he saved my life...?"

Who can forget the manner in which Baba had saved Shanta's life? It was truly astounding. Shanta was a small child then. Her father, Babu Kirwandikar, was a faithful devotee of Baba. Shanta would often accompany her parents to Dwarkamai and Baba was very fond of her. She always looked upon herself as Baba's sister.

One day, Shanta was playing alone outside her house while her mother was busy cooking the afternoon meal. Tired of playing in the same place the little child decided to go further out to explore what lay there. Her inquiring child's mind wanted to find something new to play with. She wandered further than she had ever been before. Wandering thus, she came to our village well and curiously peeped into it.

"It is so deep and big," she thought, her eyes widening in surprise. She could see the water sparkling way below as it caught the sun's rays. She stared at the water, hypnotized by its slow movement. She reached out her hands trying to catch that beautiful new toy she could see. It was so far away, but oh, so enticing. If only she stretched a little more. And then, suddenly, she lost her balance. She tumbled over and before she knew it, she had fallen in. Her frightened cry for help echoed around the deep well.

In the meanwhile, her mother was fretting. She could not see Shanta anywhere. Anxiously she called the neighbours and they set out to search for the missing girl. They searched in all the places they could think of but to no avail. Nobody had seen the little child that morning. Finally, they came to the well. Looking into it, they saw a sight they would never forget. They stood there, dumbstruck. For right there in the well was the child, balancing in mid-air, as though she was held there by an invisible hand. And indeed she was, by the hand of Baba who had heard her cry for help – although he was physically far away in Dwarkamai. There were tears in everyone's eyes as they tried to grasp the enormity of what they were seeing.

Her parents at once went to Baba with folded hands to thank him. It was truly a miracle. Everyone shuddered to think what the outcome would have been if Baba had not come to the child's aid. I remember, for days afterwards the village was buzzing with the story of Shanta's miraculous escape. With this experience the people's faith in Baba was strengthened more than ever.

"I owe Baba my life," says Shanta, misty-eyed. "He looked after us then and he will continue to look after us now."

Later, waving goodbye to Shanta, I ruminate over her words. Baba always said, "Look to me and I will look after you. That is my promise." And Baba has always kept his promise. Do we remember to keep our promises to him?

I AM THE RIVER GANGA

Janki and I step out into the bright sunshine. For years I have been visiting the village Hanuman temple on *Hanuman Jayanti* day. It is a small temple, quite ancient, with a stone statue of the Monkey God, Hanuman. There is a large crowd of people jostling for space, eager to pay obeisance to the God.

Emerging from the dark, cool interior of the temple, my eyes slowly adjust to the light outside. The narrow street is lined with roadside vendors selling articles for the *pooja* – garlands of flowers, coconuts, incense sticks and *pedhas*.

As we wend our way homewards, we meet one of our neighbours, Radhakaki. She and her son are soon to go on a pilgrimage to Pandharpur, the sacred city of Vitthala. Radhakaki had invited me to accompany them. She had tried to convince me that it would be absolutely wonderful to visit the holy temple of Vitthala. She was a little hurt when I declined her offer. I have never before travelled outside Shirdi and in all honesty I have never felt the desire to do so. With Baba in Shirdi, there was no need to look elsewhere for God.

"Laxmi, are you sure you won't change your mind?" she asks hopefully, as we stop to greet her.

"Radhakaki...." I answer but she cuts me short.

"I know, I know, the Ganga flows in Shirdi," she sighs. "Anyway, we leave tomorrow."

"Good luck for your journey," I wish her sincerely and bid her goodbye.

"What was that about the Ganga flowing in Shirdi?" asks Janki confused.

"Well, when Radhakaki tried to convince me to accompany her I told her about Das Ganu and the Ganga," I laugh. There is a puzzled look on Janki's face.

"Oh, let me tell you what happened to Das Ganu..." I commence to relate the incident to her.

Das Ganu was one of Baba's well-known disciples. One day he came to Baba with a request.

"May I go to Singba to have a dip in the holy Ganga?" he asked. You see, in this part of the world, the Godavari is referred to as the Ganga and is believed to be as sacred. Hindus believe that a dip in the Ganga river purifies all one's sins, and every Hindu tries to do so at least once in his lifetime. It is a sacred act, a means of reaching God.

But to Das Ganu's astonishment, Baba refused. He looked long and hard at Das Ganu and shook his head.

"No," he repeated.

Das Ganu was surprised. It was a simple enough request and

he had been sure that Baba would not refuse permission.

"But why not?" stammered Das Ganu, a sinking feeling in his stomach. If Baba refused permission, there was no way he would be able to fulfil his wish.

"Because you do not need to go so far," said Baba patiently.

"I do not understand Baba," said Das Ganu, perplexed. "There is no place nearer than Singba to have a dip in the Godavari."

"Why go to Singba, my friend, when the Ganga and the Jamuna are right here?" said Baba merrily, completely confusing poor Das Ganu.

Das Ganu was puzzled. Although he had tremendous faith in Baba he did not understand what Baba had said. Was he mocking him? What did he mean? Seeing his indecision Baba gently said to him, "Hold out your hands at my feet." Das Ganu obeyed hesitantly and soon water flowed out of Baba's toes and into Das Ganu's waiting hands.

Das Ganu was rendered speechless. Now everything seemed crystal clear. He finally understood Baba's message. God ultimately lived in a person's heart and mind and not in any particular place of worship or pilgrimage. Baba had beautifully demonstrated to him that one could find God sitting right where one was. Nothing is impossible for a pure, trusting heart. How true that is!

"But Radhakaki is still determined to make the pilgrimage to

Pandharpur?" asks Janki.

"I could not convince her otherwise," I answer. "It doesn't matter Janki, to each his own faith."

THE MAGIC DISHES

It is strange, the way our mind sometimes plays tricks on us. One associates certain things with people or places or events. And then these associations remind us of the most incongruous happenings. Of events which had been stashed away in some remote corner of the mind until just that moment. It happens to me all the time. I think my life had been so interwoven with Baba's, that every place I visit or everything I do has the power to bring back those jealously guarded memories of Baba.

Today it was the sight of three *fakirs* at my doorstep at noon. Hearing the chant 'Allah Malik', I came out of the house. There they were – dressed in old, torn *kafnis*, bowls in hand, to collect alms. Two of them were very young, reminding me of the young Baba who made his first appearance in Shirdi. I could almost see Baba standing there and a host of memories came flooding back.

"Allah Malik!" they shouted again, bringing me out of my reverie.

"Alms in the name of God," said the oldest of the three, very respectfully.

"Just a moment," I said and went into the kitchen to see

what I could give them. Kashinath, who had been playing in the courtyard, followed me in. Taking some of the *bhakris* and vegetable I had cooked earlier, I gave it to the *fakirs*.

"God bless you," they said and went on their way.

"Aji, there is almost nothing left for you, you will surely starve," said Kashinath doubtfully, looking at the depleted dish of vegetables.

I laughed at the worried look on his face. "Kashi, don't worry. Do you think we would ever starve with Baba looking after us?" I said.

"I know," answered Kashinath but I could see that he was not totally convinced. At this stage of his life, seeing is believing.

"Kashi, have faith in Him. That's all you need. Believe that He will always come to your aid and never forsake you. There is no bigger power than the power of faith."

"I have faith, Aji, but the dish is almost empty," said Kashinath matter-of-factly.

"Then believe that it will never be completely empty," I told him earnestly. "Kashi, have I told you about Purandarekaka's experience? It is the most unbelievable story. Maybe that will completely convince you."

"Oh do, please, Aji," answered Kashinath eagerly, always ready to hear a story.

"You, of course, know Purandarekaka," I said. Purandare was one of Baba's numerous devotees.

"Yes," he nodded.

"One day he invited Baba to his house for lunch.

'Willingly,' said Baba, 'but make sure you prepare enough lunch for two or three more *fakirs*.'

Purandare happily went home and told his wife that Baba was to come to their house for lunch the following day with a few other *fakirs*. His wife, as excited as Purandare, set about getting everything organised for the big day.

The next day a sumptuous meal was ready by mid-day. As Purandare waited for Baba, five *fakirs* came in, informing Purandare that they had come on Baba's instructions for the afternoon meal. Purandare welcomed them into his home and served them lunch. As they left, they informed him that some more *fakirs* had been directed by Baba to partake of lunch at Purandare's house. Soon, a group of 20 *fakirs* arrived. Purandare was greatly alarmed. His wife had cooked enough food for five *fakirs*. How was he to feed another 20?

A panic-stricken Purandare quickly requested her to cook some more food so that none of Baba's friends would go hungry.

His wife was appalled. Her husband was asking her to produce a meal in minutes. 'How can I cook a full meal in such a short time?' said the poor, flustered lady, almost in tears.

'Hurry, do whatever you can,' pleaded her husband.

Going into the kitchen, his wife said a quick prayer to Baba. 'Please Baba, help me out of this difficulty, help me feed all your friends today,' she prayed earnestly. To her utter amazement, on opening the dishes of food she found they were all full to the brim. Her prayer had been answered!

Seconds later, an astounded Purandare saw his wife rush out in a state of great excitement and confidently announce, 'Invite as many *fakirs* as you like, I can feed them all.'

Purandare and his wife fed the 20 *fakirs*. Soon another group of *fakirs* arrived with Baba. But there was no shortage of food — the dishes were constantly magically refilled! And all the guests were well fed and satisfied.

As Baba rose to leave, Purandare and his wife knelt before him with great devotion and humility. 'Baba,' they said, 'Bless us that we may forever know thy grace.'

'In whatever faith men worship me, even so do I render to them,' said Baba solemnly. 'Know that my eye is ever on those who love me.'

So you see Kashi, just have faith in Baba. That's all he asks for, faith and patience, and in exchange he gives you everything."

A DREAM COME TRUE

It was the festival of Holi. In the early hours of the morning, Govindpant Dabholkar had a dream. Baba, dressed as a *sanyasi,* shook him awake and said, "Today, I shall come to you for a meal."

When Dabholkar woke up, he felt elated. Of course, he could not see Baba but he tried to recollect his dream and remember Baba's exact words. He went over them and was convinced that his dream would translate into reality.

With that firm conviction he told his wife to cook some extra rice that day. "Why?" she wanted to know.

"We have a guest for lunch today," answered Dabholkar, trying not to reveal anything more.

"Who is the guest?" his wife inquired curiously.

Dabholkar tried to dodge her questions, not wanting to appear naïve. After much persistence on her part, he finally narrated his dream to her. "Baba will have lunch with us today," he ended, with utmost confidence.

His wife stared at him skeptically. "Surely you don't believe, based on a mere dream that Baba will come to our home for a meal?" she asked, incredulous.

"I do," answered her husband, unshaken. "He may not be one whom we recognize as Baba but he will surely be present in some form or another. He would not have given me such an assurance otherwise."

His wife shook her head disbelievingly and rolled her eyes. "Why would he leave Shirdi and come here?" she persisted.

"He does not need to leave Shirdi. Baba can be present in different places at the same time. And all I am asking you to do is to cook an extra measure of rice," Dabholkar said, putting an end to the conversation.

Holi is a colourful festival. The day commenced with gaiety. Festive decorations were put up in the house, intricate and colourful *rangolis* were drawn and offerings were made to the Holi fire. The kitchen was a hub of activity, the women of the house bracing themselves to feed all the invited relatives and guests. A special wooden seat was reserved for Baba and a plate of food was served.

At 12 noon, all the guests took their seats to start lunch. Only Baba's seat was empty. Everyone waited expectantly for the special guest to arrive. The seconds ticked by slowly but nobody showed up. Unable to keep his guests waiting any longer, Dabholkar decided to commence with the meal. He sadly closed the main door to the house after taking one last lingering look outside. He sat down with his guests and requested them to partake of lunch. Grace was then said. Just as Dabholkar was about to put the first morsel of food into his mouth, there was a loud knock on the door. Dabholkar got up to answer it. On opening the door, he found two gentlemen outside. One of them was Ali Mohammad, a disciple of Baba; the other, Ismu Mujawar. Ali Mohammad carried a parcel wrapped in newspaper, under his arm. Taking in the scene before him, he said, "I am so sorry to intrude at a time like this. I have just come to give you this," and so saying, he started to unwrap the parcel under his arm. "I will tell you the marvelous tale behind this at a more opportune time," he continued. Finally unwrapping the last layer of newspaper, Ali Mohammad triumphantly held up a beautiful statuette of Baba. "This is for you," he said simply, handing the statuette to Dabholkar.

Dabholkar could not believe his eyes. With a trembling hand, he took the statuette, gazing at it with awe. He looked at Ali Mohammad through a film of tears, thanking him from the bottom of his heart.

"We must take your leave now," Ali Mohammad said. "I will explain it all another time."

Dabholkar was anyway too overcome to ask anything further. He lovingly placed the statuette on the seat reserved for Baba. His dream had been realized; more importantly, his faith had been rewarded. "Baba did not fail me," his heart sang joyfully.

Dabholkar was eager to know the story behind the appearance of the statuette. However, the origin of the statuette and its journey to its destination remained a mystery to him for a long time. It seemed to him that his question would never be answered, for Ali Mohammad and Ismu Mujawar appeared to have vanished. However, what mattered to Dabholkar was that it had arrived just in time. He simply accepted it as a symbol of Baba's grace and munificence.

Nine years passed thus, without any meeting with either of the two men. Until one day, Dabholkar unexpectedly encountered Ali Mohammad on the street. They greeted each other warmly and then Dabholkar said, "My friend, long have I waited to hear the tale of the statuette. Tell me all, now."

And Ali Mohammad replied, "Very well. I can understand your eagerness. Listen to my words, for I am going to relate an incredible tale indeed.

One day, as I was walking in the streets of Bombay, my attention was caught by some beautiful paintings and statuettes of saints. I stopped to look at them and as I went through the collection, I saw this exquisitely delicate statuette of which we speak. Moreover, being a statuette of Baba, it appealed to me and I bought it at once. I took it home and hung it up on the wall.

Well, a few months before I came to your home, I was quite ill. My leg had to be operated upon and it was a difficult time for me. I lived alone and drew great strength from the photographs and statuettes of the saints that adorned my wall. The statuette of Baba, in particular, gave me great comfort. One of the photographs occupying pride of place on my wall was that of Baba Abdul Rehman. This was given to me by my brother-in-law who was his disciple. My brother-in-law, in his enthusiasm, had got many copies made of the photograph and had distributed them to all his friends and relatives. Then, with great devotion, he presented one photograph to Baba Abdul Rehman. He stood before his Guru, smiling, waiting for his kind words and blessing. But to his dismay, Baba Abdul Rehman raged at him. Instead of kind words, he was showered with a barrage of harsh accusations; in place of blessing, he was rebuked and sent off the premises. 'A Muslim did not worship photographs and idols,' he was repudiated. 'Had he lost his way?'

Utterly dejected and remorseful at having infuriated his Guru, my brother-in-law went home. He was a devout Muslim and wanted to be true to his Guru. He collected all the photographs he had and immersed them in the sea. I was then living in his house and he said to me, 'It is bad luck to keep these photographs in the house. See how they made me incur my Guru's displeasure. I am sure your illness has been caused by your errant behaviour. Your collection of statuettes and photographs increases all the time. Get rid of them all and eliminate your troubles."

On hearing his earnest appeal, I called my assistant. Since I was still immobile, I instructed him to go to my home and take all the photographs and statuettes off my wall. Following my instructions faithfully, my assistant gave them to my brother-in-law to do as he willed with them. My brother-in-law took a ferry boat out to sea and immersed the entire lot.

When I recovered, about two months later, I went to my own home. On opening the door, I stood shell-shocked, for facing me on the wall, was the exquisite statuette of Baba. I looked around and found that not one of the other statuettes or photographs had survived the cleansing. Only Baba still remained on my wall, greeting me as I entered. 'Why was this statuette left here?' I wondered. 'How did it escape the notice of my assistant?' Baba chooses to stay where he wills, I thought in awe; the dictates of uncomprehending minds have no power over him.

But I had no wish to agitate my brother-in-law. So I carefully took down the statuette myself and hid it in a cupboard. I felt uncomfortable doing that. A statuette of Baba was not to be consigned to the dark environs of a musty cupboard; his glory was meant to be shared with others. I decided that the best way out was to give it away to someone. I was anxious that the recipient be one who would cherish it as much as I did and the only person who came to mind was you. I had known you long enough to perceive the love you carried in your heart for Baba. I felt you were the only one to whom I could entrust such a precious possession. Ismu Mujawar reaffirmed my belief and that is how we came to your house on that day."

Dabholkar made no attempt to hide the tears streaming from his eyes. "Ali Mohammad," he said, "you did more than entrust something valuable to me. You were a messenger from Baba." And he narrated the story of his dream.

It was Ali Mohammad's turn to get emotional. "Allah Malik," he said chokingly. "Baba's *leela* is remarkable."

BABA PROVES THE ASTROLOGER WRONG

We are always told that everything is in the mind. Our mind is all-powerful. It is our mind that can help us surmount the most difficult obstacles or drag us down into the throes of depression. It is our mind that makes us aspire to some of the greatest things in life and the same mind makes us commit the most terrible acts. But our mind is not like a pliant pet dog that obeys orders. It seems to have an agenda of its own. "How does one learn to control the mind?" I often asked Baba. Baba would reply, "If you surrender your mind to the Guru and have faith in Him, your mind will become your greatest ally."

Let me narrate to you an amazing story about faith and the power of the mind.

It is about a boy called Babu Tendulkar. Babu was a medical student and that year he was to appear for his final year medical examination. Babu studied hard as he had always done, wanting to do well in the final examination.

Now it so happened, that shortly before the examination, an astrologer visited Babu's parents. He looked long and hard at Babu and then made an awful prediction: Babu would not pass his final examination! On hearing this, Babu was at first alarmed and then he became very depressed. "What is the use of studying anymore if I am going to fail?" he thought to himself. And so, he did the worst thing he could do – he stopped studying.

This greatly troubled Babu's mother. She was very worried, seeing her son so dejected and neglectful of his studies. She tried to explain to Babu that he should not take the astrologer's words so seriously. But Babu's mind was in turmoil. Babu's mind had decided to believe the astrologer.

Babu's mother had great faith in Baba. "I must seek Baba's help," she thought. "He is our only hope."

When Baba heard what had happened he advised Babu to study as usual and to have faith in Him. "Do not believe what people tell you," he said. " Study well, have faith and appear for the examination – you will do well."

The medical examination was in two parts, written and practical. At first Babu followed Baba's advice and appeared for the written examination. But the astrologer's words echoed in his head and he got more and more afraid that the prediction would come true. How humiliating it would be, his mind told him, if he did not get through the examination. What would people say? What would his friends think? Oh, it was too terrible to contemplate. His mind was in turmoil. He could not concentrate on his studies and finally, he took a decision. He would not appear for the practical examination that was to take place two days later. He could not battle the negative thoughts he had. His mind had convinced him that he had failed!

And then, an unheard of thing happened on the day of the practical examination. Babu was actually summoned by the Examiner to find out why he was not present.

"Because I have surely failed the written examination," replied Babu, hanging his head in shame.

"Failed?" said the Examiner, astonished. "My dear boy, what makes you say that? You have most definitely passed the written exam."

Babu's amazement knew no bounds. He at once appeared for the practical examination and sure enough, passed with good marks. The astrologer had been proved wrong.

"I should have had faith in Baba and not the astrologer," thought Babu to himself, deciding never to doubt Baba again.

Later, Baba spoke to him good words of counsel. "There is tremendous power in our mind, Babu," he said, "Never underestimate it. We can make our mind our ally or our enemy; the decision is entirely up to us. The best way to make a friend of our mind is to surrender it at the feet of the Guru and let him control it."

With Baba as our Guru, we need not ever worry about the path our mind will take.

SAVED FROM THE FLAMES

I have been sitting before the *choolah* cooking the afternoon meal. As I stoke the fire, I feel myself almost hypnotized by the flames. Fire can be so beautiful in all its leaping, vibrant shades but how dangerous too! What it would have done to that poor little child on that fateful day if Baba had not performed a most remarkable feat! It is an awful thought. But Baba saved the infant daughter of our village smith from the wrath of the flames.

It happened a few years ago. She was just a little baby. Her mother had been carrying her in her arms, blowing the fire in the forge. Soon the child's father arrived and called out to her mother. In her haste to attend to him, the mother's grip on the wriggling child loosened and she fell into the fire. Her mother could only scream in terror as she watched her baby descend into the flames.

At that same instant in Dwarkamai, Baba was standing before the *dhuni,* adding logs of wood to the fire. Some devotees, including Shama, his close disciple, were also present. All of a sudden Baba thrust his hand into the hot, burning fire, his eyes fixed on some distant spot. Everyone was aghast. What was Baba doing? They rushed up to him and dragged him away from the fire. Baba seemed to be in a trance. As his badly scorched hand was pulled out of the fire, he returned to the present.

"Oh Baba, what have you done?" asked Shama, in a pained voice. "Why put your hand in a raging fire and inflict injury upon yourself?"

Baba's hand was indeed in a terrible condition. There was a faraway look in his eyes.

"Shama," he answered softly, "How could I let that poor infant be scorched by the flames? Better my hand than that little baby."

"What infant, Baba?" asked Shama puzzled.

"The village smith's little baby girl, Shama" answered Baba. "As her mother stoked the flames, she fell out of her arms into the fire. What could I do? I had to pick her up and save her life." There was a look of immense relief and compassion on Baba's face as he spoke.

Baba saved that innocent young life at the cost of incurring much pain. But isn't that the sign of a true Guru? One who takes on the suffering of others regardless of the cost to himself? Someone who is loving and compassionate, relieving others of their pain and granting them succour?

As I continue sitting before the fire, I repeat to myself Baba's words, "Once you entrust yourself to the hands of the *sadguru*, you do not have to worry. I never forsake anyone who relies on me." Baba has never failed his devotees.

Dixit Wada

BACK FROM THE DEAD

Late last night, Ramukaka, the oldest person in our village, passed away. The funeral took place on the banks of the Godavari River.

"What is death, Aji? Does it mean that Ramukaka will never come back again?" asks Kashinath, perturbed.

"Yes Kashi, death is final. No one comes back from the dead," I explain gently to him.

"Unless," I think to myself, "Baba wills otherwise." Remembering one such incident, my hair stands on end. When the *sadguru* wills otherwise, death dare not inflict any blow on the devotee.

It was a tug of war between a little girl on the one hand and the God of Death on the other. Who would emerge victorious? The child had complete and unshakeable faith in Baba but Death seemed all ready to snatch her away.

It happened that this little girl suddenly fell seriously ill. Her parents were alarmed and at once consulted the doctor. "I'm afraid your daughter has tuberculosis," said the doctor sadly.

TB is a fatal disease without any cure. Thousands of people die of TB due to lack of medicines. Hopefully one day a cure will be found for this dreaded disease. Naturally, the girl's parents were very upset and worried about their daughter. Why did their little girl have to suffer so? Why was she to be snatched away from them? They tried everything they could to find a cure. Every doctor was consulted, every remedy was tried. No stone was left unturned. Anything and everything was worth trying if only their precious child could be saved. But alas, they did not meet with any success.

But the little girl would not give up. She had full confidence in Baba and in her heart she felt sure that he would not fail her. She believed in him totally, believed that he was her only refuge.

"Please take me to Baba," she begged her parents.

"But you are too weak to travel!" protested her mother.

"Please mother," she pleaded. "I must see him. I know he will cure me."

So her parents took her to Shirdi. The journey was long and tiring but the little girl was happy. She was finally going to Baba. In Shirdi, they stayed with their friends the Dixits. When Baba was informed of the arrival of the girl in Shirdi, a strange smile played on his lips. A host of expressions crossed his face – compassion, love, determination. "Allah Malik," he whispered looking heavenwards.

The next day, Baba came to see the girl who had so trustingly placed her life in his hands. Looking at that lovely innocent child, his kind eyes were full of love. He tenderly placed his hand on her head. The child felt a sudden sense of calm descend upon her.

"Let her sleep on a blanket and do not give her anything other than water," he instructed her parents. That day she slept peacefully, like she had not slept in a long time.

Baba's orders were faithfully obeyed for a whole week. But her condition remained the same. The high fever and weakness continued. She still did not seem to be recovering. Her illness was not abating. But at least, thought her parents, her condition was not deteriorating. And the child seemed much more comfortable.

And then, on the eighth day, a terrible thing happened. Early in the morning the girl passed away. Everyone was shocked and dismayed. This was not possible. She had believed in Baba and entrusted her life to him. How could Baba let this happen to her? Why could he not have saved her? Why had he given her parents false hopes? Upset and hurt, the parents went to Dwarkamai to inform Baba about the girl's death. Surprisingly they found him still fast asleep although he was normally an early riser.

However in a short while, Baba woke up and started behaving in the strangest manner. He jumped up and rushed around. He started ranting and raving and waving his hands about. He screamed and shouted at someone...someone whom only he seemed to be able to see. There was nobody there. He charged out of Dwarkamai and out on to the street, behaving as strange as ever. Had Baba lost his mind, wondered everybody, trying to get out of his way as quickly as possible.

Baba then ran towards Dixit Wada shouting and hitting the ground with a stick as though he was chasing someone away. Someone unwanted, someone unwelcome. The God of Death, perhaps?

As people watched, half amused, half afraid, they heard shouts coming from Dixit Wada.

"The girl is alive! She has come back from the dead!"

DISTANCE IS NO BARRIER

This morning the village postman Sayyadbhai hailed Narsimha as he passed him on the street. He rummaged in his brown cloth sack until he found what he was looking for.

"I have a letter for Aji," he told Narsimha, handing him an envelope. "Make sure you give it to her."

The letter is from my cousin in Sindon. She has written to inform me of a forthcoming marriage in the family next month. It has taken the letter three weeks to arrive in Shirdi.

"Aji, wouldn't it be wonderful if we knew everything that went on everywhere, like Baba? Then we would not need to wait so long to receive news," says Narsimha, his eyes shining with excitement.

"Indeed Narsimha, it would be very, very nice. But you and I do not have quite the same powers as Baba did!" I answer, amused at the thought.

"I know," he says frowning. "But if I could," he continues, his eyes twinkling with mischief, "I would know exactly what tricks Saru and Kashi were up to. I would also know what the schoolmaster was doing. Wouldn't that be great Aji, just think, I would never get into trouble!"

His childish delight is quite infectious. I wonder myself, what it would be like to be able to see and know all, sitting in just one place. Baba had the amazing power to be all-knowing without even leaving Dwarkamai. He had the power to manifest himself in different forms and different places at the same time. But then, Baba was one of those rare beings that had reached a very high level of consciousness. Many were those who experienced his unique power. Amongst them were Ramchandra (Babasaheb) Tarkhad and his son, both men totally devoted to Baba. There is an interesting tale involving these two devotees.

The Tarkhads lived in a suburb of Mumbai called Bandra. Living so far away from Shirdi, they had installed in their home, a framed portrait of Baba. Everyday, very religiously, the son worshipped the portrait after the morning bath. Babasaheb did not believe in ritualistic worship but his son did. He commenced his daily activities only after performing *pooja* and offering *naivedya* consisting of sugar. He was very particular about following this ritual every day and did not eat a morsel of food until Baba had been offered food first in the form of *naivedya.*

One day, Babasaheb's wife expressed her desire to visit Shirdi and meet Baba. She requested her son to accompany her. The son was ever ready to go to Shirdi but he was concerned about the daily *pooja* and *naivedya* ritual. Would his father follow it in his absence?

Clearly reading the turmoil in his son's mind, Babasaheb said to him "Son, go to Shirdi with an easy mind. I will make sure that Baba is offered *naivedya* daily."

Greatly assured by his father's words, the boy accompanied his mother to Shirdi.

After his son's departure, Babasaheb conscientiously performed the *pooja* everyday and offered *naivedya* to Baba. This went on for many days and all was well.

Then one day, inadvertently, the lapse occurred. Babasaheb had some urgent business to attend to and in his haste he forgot to offer *naivedya* to Baba. On returning home in the afternoon he realized his mistake. Babasaheb felt guilty and remorseful. His son had relied on him to perform this daily ritual and he had let him down. Even worse, he had forgotten to feed Baba that day. He prostrated himself before the portrait of Baba and begged forgiveness. "Baba, I have sinned, forgive me," he pleaded.

In his misery, he wrote a letter to his son in Shirdi, telling him about his folly and asking him to beg Baba's forgiveness on his behalf.

Now, amazingly, while this chain of events was unfolding in a Mumbai suburb, there was something equally astounding happening in Shirdi. On that same day, Mrs Tarkhad and her son went to Dwarkamai for Baba's *darshan*. Baba was in conversation with some devotees, a benign look upon his face. Mother and son approached him and bowed down reverently. As they stood before him, Baba said, "O Mother, today I went to your house in Bandra as usual. But there was nothing for me to eat or drink and I had to return hungry." On hearing Baba's words, the boy's heart sank. He realized that something had gone wrong with the *naivedya* ritual that day. In all probability his father had forgotten. "Why, oh, why did I entrust this to him?" thought the boy, wretchedly. Feeling very ashamed and unhappy, he asked for Baba's forgiveness. But Baba, the fount of compassion, gently said , "Rise my son, do not torment yourself. Today, you may offer me the *naivedya* here itself."

Greatly cheered, the boy performed the ritual then and there. The same day he wrote a detailed letter to his father, telling him what had transpired.

Later, as father and son read each other's letters they were absolutely stupefied. Baba knew what went on in Bandra when he was miles away in Shirdi! Baba's divine power truly transcended boundaries and distance. Although he appeared never to leave Shirdi, he was, in fact, everywhere at the same time. The thought itself was astounding. Their hearts overflowing with love, the Tarkhads counted themselves blessed to have Baba for their Guru. No matter what, he would always, in some form or the other, be with his devotees.

COMPASSION

Saru came into my home this morning, sobbing furiously. "Whatever is the matter, child?" I questioned, at once worried. She clung to me, hugging me around the waist, her face buried into my shoulder. I let her cry awhile before turning her face up to look at me. Her swollen eyes slowly stopped shedding tears and she calmed down.

"What is it, Saru?" I asked again, wiping her face with the end of my sari pallav.

"It was horrible, Aji," she cried, "they were stoning him."

"Stoning whom? Who was?" I queried.

"There was a leper at the market, begging alms. He looked horrible Aji, with cloth bandages tied around his face and hands. As he went from person to person, he happened to bump into one of the fruit vendors. The vendor went hysterical, claiming that he would get infected with leprosy. Soon, a crowd gathered and started throwing stones at the poor man," she shuddered.

"Oh no," I exclaimed, horrified. "Didn't anybody stop them?"

"A few people did try but the mob seemed to see red. They

wanted him to be punished for touching the vendor. So they continued stoning him cruelly," Saru started crying again. "It was so gruesome, Aji.... so heartless. I couldn't bear to see him, surrounded by that vengeful crowd."

My heart went out to the unfortunate man, so shabbily treated by the world. When would people change their warped thinking and learn to be compassionate to others not as fortunate as themselves?

"Aji, is it true that one is infected by the mere touch of a leper?" asks Saru.

"No, child, that is not correct. What is more, one should feel compassion for the sick and ailing. They are in so much pain, physically and emotionally, that it is important to treat them with kindness. Never harbour such negative thoughts about people, Saru. Come, sit down, I want to tell you a little story."

Saru wiped her eyes and sat opposite me on the cool floor.

"This is a beautiful, touching story, Saru. You know that Baba always treated everyone equally, whether he was a Brahmin or a beggar. Well, in Baba's world, lepers were given the same regard as anyone else.

One day, at Dwarkamai, Baba was in the company of his disciples. Amongst them, was Tarabai Tarkhad, a devoted follower of Baba. Some time went by, and then, a figure was seen approaching the *masjid*. It was a man with an emaciated body, carrying a cloth bundle on his back. He walked slowly, halting every now and again to catch his breath. When he reached the steps to Dwarkamai, he was clearly visible. He had leprosy. His disease was already in an advanced state, his sores were oozing and there was a terrible stench about him. He started to climb up the few steps to the *masjid*, wincing with pain. People looked at him warily, some with pity, others with horror.

Finally, with a great deal of effort, the man neared Baba. Reaching his destination, he placed his cloth bundle on the floor and rested his head on Baba's feet. 'Allah Malik' said Baba, placing a tender hand on the man's head. The leper looked gratefully up at Baba, clearly joyful to receive the loving glance from Baba's gentle eyes. Tarabai watched him too but her eyes only reflected her disgust. She was clearly revolted at what she saw. 'Baba did not have to entertain all and sundry,' she thought.

There was silence in Dwarkamai, everyone watching the diseased man. He did not seem at all concerned about the reactions he evoked. He only gazed upon Baba, finding comfort in the presence of the Master. Then, having accomplished his mission, he picked up his little bundle and began to retrace his steps. As he started to climb down, Tarabai mentally heaved a sigh of relief. 'Thank God the man would be off soon, taking his stench and sores with him,' she thought uncharitably. No sooner had the thought entered her head, than Baba turned to look piercingly at her. All of a sudden, he stood up and called the leper back. The poor man again shuffled up painstakingly, not knowing why he had been thus summoned. Baba smiled kindly at him. 'Please open your bundle,' he told the surprised man. The man set to work to untie his dirty cloth bundle which, on opening, revealed some *pedhas*. Baba took a piece of *pedha* and offered it to Tarabai. In spite of the fact that there were other people around, he offered the *pedha* only to Tarabai. The flustered lady had no choice but to accept it. Hesitating for a few seconds, she finally ate it! Baba then took another piece and ate it himself."

There was a gasp from Saru. "Well," I asked her smiling, "what do you think of this story?"

"It must have been an unforgettable lesson for Tarabai, Aji," she answered slowly.

"Yes it was. Baba always had a unique way of conveying his message Saru. And he practiced what he preached. Although he made Tarabai eat a piece of the *pedha*, he himself ate some too. It was a very effective way of conveying some truths and teaching the simple values of compassion and equality."

"Aji," said Saru suddenly as a thought struck her, "did not Bhagoji have leprosy?"

"That is right, Saru." Bhagoji was Baba's disciple and one of the few persons present when Baba gave up his mortal body. His disease had never mattered to Baba. In fact, Bhagoji was the only one allowed to care for Baba when his arm had been burnt in saving the village smith's child.

"Do you remember the story of the little girl who was saved by Baba from the flames of the fire? Baba's arm was very badly burnt then. He, of course, did not make much of it, but it worried us. Bhagoji began to apply *ghee* to it and bandage it daily. Baba would let nobody but Bhagoji dress his wound."

"Baba had a special empathy for people who were suffering, isn't it? I hope he is looking out for that poor man who got stoned today," Saru murmured. "He must be in great distress."

"Pray for him," I told her. "Baba will surely help him."

AN HEIR FOR RATANJI

The children have just left my home to go to bed. Suddenly, my house falls sadly silent. They have become such an integral part of my life, I cannot imagine being without them. I find an energizing, innocent equation in their company; much laughter and mischievous interludes. A certain freshness too, which brings a happy perspective to my life. I can understand the longing of those childless couples who would come to Baba, asking to be blessed with progeny. I begin to recall the joy on the face of Ratanji when his son was born....

Seth Ratanji Shapoorji Wadia, a Parsi gentleman of Nanded was a wealthy mill contractor. He was an extremely religious and god-fearing man and was well respected by all. He led a very comfortable life, owning a fair amount of property that included vast estates, farms, carriages and other assets. Extremely generous by nature, he was very charitable, always ready to have others share in his abundance. Ratanji Seth, then, was a happy man, but not quite. You see, Ratanji Seth had twelve daughters but no son. He loved all his daughters dearly but he yearned for a male child; a healthy boy to carry on the family name and take over the weight of running the family business from his aging shoulders.

In his sadness, Ratanji worried greatly; he was tormented. He prayed to God but his prayers went unanswered. Then, one day, Ratanji expressed his sorrow to his friend, Das Ganu, a disciple of Baba. Das Ganu said to him, "Go to Shirdi and seek Baba's blessings. Your wish will surely be fulfilled."

Some time later, Ratanji went to Shirdi. He prostrated himself at Baba's feet, saying, "I have come to you, in all humility, to seek your Grace. You never turn away anyone who comes to you. Grant me the one thing I desire more than anything in this world. You are the only one who can give me that joy."

Baba looked at him kindly and said in a gentle voice, "So you have finally come here. Where is my *dakshina*?"

Baba would often ask for d*akshina,* which is an offering of money made to holy persons. As a renunciate, Baba did not need any money but there was a much deeper significance to his actions. The wealthy and the poor were both asked for *dakshina*. The amounts too, differed. A wealthy man was sometimes asked for a paltry sum of money whereas a poor man was asked for a substantial amount. There were many significant reasons behind the request for *dakshina*. Often, it was to free the devotee from some past, forgotten debt. When people are in dire trouble, they make vows to God, promising all sorts of things in thanksgiving if they are freed of their worries. And then, when all is well again, they forget to fulfill their obligation. Baba would remind the devotee of his past promises, made in times of difficulty. By asking for *dakshina*, he would free the person from debt. The soul also accumulates debts from one lifetime to another, in the karmic cycle of birth and death. Gurus like Baba, who shepherd their flock from birth to birth, help their disciples redeem promises and debts of a birth hitherto unknown to the disciple. The ways of saints are therefore often incomprehensible. They guide their followers, helping them overcome all obstacles in their way and set them on to the right path. *Dakshina* was also a way of creating humility in the disciple, a means of instruction in charity. One was encouraged to give to another, because when one gives, one receives two-fold. Baba was above material and sensory pleasures. He had no use for the *dakshina* he collected; he would in turn give it away to others.

When Baba asked him for *dakshina*, Ratanji at once put his hand in his pocket to take out some money. Just then, Baba intriguingly said to him, "You have earlier given me 3 rupees and 14 *annas*. Now you can give me the balance *dakshina*."

Ratanji was puzzled. This was his first visit to Shirdi. He could not recollect having sent Baba any money in the past either. He pondered Baba's mysterious statement…"3 rupees and 14 *annas*…"

Ratanji proceeded to give Baba *dakshina*. He was still pondering Baba's words but did not pursue the matter. With total devotion he said to Baba, "O Baba, you are all-knowing, I am but your simple follower. You know what grieves me, what causes me so much bitter anguish. Remove that impediment with your Grace, Baba. I have come to seek refuge in you."

Baba was touched by the sincere pain in Ratanji's plea. He gave him some *udi* and placing his hand on his head, gently said, "Fret no more. Your wish shall be fulfilled."

Back in Nanded, Ratanji recounted the events of Shirdi to

Das Ganu. He expressed the joy he felt in Baba's presence and the wonderful assurance he had received. "But there was one thing that did not fall into place," he went on.

"What was that?" Das Ganu asked.

"Well, Baba asked for *dakshina* and insisted that I had earlier given him 3 rupees and 14 *annas*. How could that be possible? This was my very first visit to Shirdi, I had never met Baba before this. It does not make any sense to me, Das Ganu," the perplexed Ratanji continued.

Das Ganu, too, thought deeply but was unable to fathom Baba's cryptic words. And then, he suddenly remembered. "Maulisaheb!" he exclaimed, "How much money did you spend on the meal for Maulisaheb?"

Maulisaheb was a muslim saint, well loved by the people of Nanded. Ratanji, too, treated him with great reverence. Das Ganu remembered that before Ratanji left for Shirdi, Maulisaheb had visited his home and had been served a meal. "How much did you spend, Ratanji?" he queried excitedly.

Ratanji promptly began to calculate the expenses of that meal. To his great astonishment, the total came to exactly 3 rupees and 14 *annas*! He was absolutely amazed. Realized souls are truly part of one consciousness, no matter where they are. Living physically in Shirdi, Baba knew all the events that transpired everywhere. He had reached a level where he was omnipresent and omniscient!

On a lovely sunny day, less than a year from the date he visited

Shirdi, Ratanji's cup of joy overflowed; he became the proud father of a healthy baby boy. Ratanji's heart was filled with love and gratitude for Baba. His wish had indeed been fulfilled; Baba's blessing had fructified. Later, in the years to come, Ratanji was blessed with more sons and his happiness knew no bounds. He thereafter regularly visited Shirdi, seeking Baba's Grace and guidance, grateful to have the privilege of his Master's presence.

I HAVE MANY FORMS

The big grey and white cat suddenly jumps off the roof into the courtyard. She has smelt the milk that Janki has poured out for Kashinath in a little glass on the threshold. Kashinath promptly proceeds to chase her away. She runs off and perches herself on the wall. Preening herself in the sun she feigns total disinterest in the milk.

"Kashi, drink up the milk before Rani helps herself to it," I warn, seeing the cat eyeing the pail.

"Let her just try," announces Kashinath, picking up a few stones to hurl at the cat. The first stone misses her completely, the second almost grazes her leg.

"Stop, Kashi," I admonish him, "Don't throw stones at that poor creature."

"Why not?" he asks adamantly. "She wants to drink the milk – but its for me!"

"She won't now," I tell him, bringing out a special dish of milk for Rani and placing it outside. "She has her own dish of milk. But anyway Kashi, you should never hurt any creature."

Rani jumps down from the wall in a flash and makes straight for the milk. Within seconds she has lapped it up. She retraces her steps to the wall and stretches out indolently in the sun.

"Why do you always feed her Aji? She doesn't belong to you," asks Kashinath.

"Kashi, one must be kind to animals. They are also part of life and deserve to be treated well."

"Do they have the same feelings as us, Aji?" asks Kashinath, curiously.

"I'm sure they do. In fact, if they could speak they could tell us a lot. You know, Kashi, Baba used to always say that when you are cruel to an animal or any living creature, you are actually hurting him. He was always so compassionate towards animals."

Telling Kashi about Baba's kindness to animals, I recall the simple way in which Baba once taught me such an important lesson. I feel like imparting that same lesson to little Kashi.

"You know, Kashi, one day I had gone to Dwarkamai. On seeing me, Baba promptly said, 'Laxmi, I am very hungry.'

'I will prepare some fresh *bhakris* for you Baba,' I told him and immediately went back home.

I roasted some *bhakris* and packed them along with some vegetable and rushed back to Dwarkamai, all the while unable to bear the thought of Baba being hungry."

"He must have been happy to get fresh *bhakris* Aji," says Kashi. "Was he ?"

"Yes, he was, Kashi," I answer wistfully. "But do you know what he did?"

"What, Aji?" he asks curiously.

"There was a dog lying nearby. As soon as I placed the food before Baba, he picked it up and put it before the dog."

"Oh no!" says Kashi, aghast.

"Yes Kashi, I was horrified too. And very hurt. I had rushed home and hastily roasted fresh *bhakris* for Baba and he didn't seem to appreciate it."

"Baba," I said, tears in my eyes, "I had prepared these for you with so much devotion because you were hungry. You did not eat even a tiny piece. Instead you gave them away to a mongrel! And do you know what Baba said to me Kashi? He explained something to me that I will never forget."

"What did he say?" asks Kashinath eagerly.

" 'Laxmi,' he said kindly, 'I was hungry and you brought me food. But why do you say I did not eat it? Isn't this dog also part of this life force? Part of me? In feeding him, you feed me. His hunger is the same as mine.'

I looked at him, feeling ashamed of my earlier reaction. Seeing my anguish he continued gently, 'Do not distress yourself, child. There is nothing greater than relieving the hunger of another. When you feed any creature, you feed me.' He paused, giving me a lovely smile. 'Laxmi,' he said, filling my heart with joy, 'you have fed me today through this dog. Your kindness shall be remembered.' "

Kashi is gazing at me with a serious look on his face. He seems to have understood the message of the story.

"Kashi, do you want to hear a funny story about this?" I ask him.

"Sure Aji," says Kashinath, his interest aroused at once.

"Well, it is a story related to me by Mrs. Tarkhad, Babasaheb's wife. She was on a visit to Shirdi. It was noon. She had made her way to the dining hall. Food was being served to all who were seated there. As she was about to begin her meal, a stray dog came by. He stopped near her and looked at her expectantly. 'He looks hungry,' thought the kind lady and she promptly gave him a piece of *bhakri* from her *thali*. The dog eagerly picked it up and went on his way. Mrs Tarkhad continued with her meal.

Soon thereafter, a pig came by covered in mud and filth. He made his way to many of the people seated there. Most of them just shooed him away heartlessly, not happy to have the filthy, smelly creature come near them. When he came near her, the lady kindly gave him a piece of *bhakri* too. The pig grabbed it and looked at her. In spite of all the layers of dirt and mud on his body, his eyes were clear. He gave his benefactress a look of gratitude and then went away. Mrs

Tarkhad finished the remainder of her lunch. She did not give her actions much thought and went on with other things in the day.

Later that day, she went to Dwarkamai for Baba's *darshan*. There was, as usual, a group of people seated there. She bowed down and sat herself down at some distance from Baba. After a while Baba looked piercingly at her and said 'Thank you mother, for feeding me so well today. I was suffering great pangs of hunger and you fed me.'

Mrs Tarkhad could not understand what Baba was saying. Maybe he was talking to someone else. She looked behind her but there was no one sitting there. The poor lady tried desperately to recall the events of the day. Was she losing her memory? She could not recall serving Baba any food that day. She had not even visited Dwarkamai until then. She wondered what he was talking about. What could she say? She did not want to offend him.

'Baba,' she said a trifle hesitantly, 'I did not feed you today.'

'Oh but you did, unknowingly,' Baba insisted. 'While you were having lunch today you fed the passing dog and the filthy pig. Who do you think they were?'

'You mean,' began Mrs Tarkhad wonderingly ...

'I mean that I am one with all living creatures. Sometimes I am a dog, sometimes a pig and sometimes an insect. One must learn to treat them all alike for they are all part of life's divine force. Always have compassion for those in need of food. Feed them first and then yourself. You shall be blessed for your kindness and compassion today,' he added, smiling gently at her.

Hearing Baba speak these words the lady rejoiced in her heart. Blessed indeed was she who was blessed thus by Baba.

And so, my dear Kashi, remember that we are all part of nature and must treat our fellow creatures kindly, whatever they be."

"Aji," asks Kashinath looking troubled, "when I threw stones at Rani, I, in fact, threw stones at Baba, didn't I?"

I can see that he is greatly perturbed. "Yes, Kashi but it doesn't matter as long as you learn from your mistakes."

He thinks for a moment, a frown creasing his brow. "Aji, may I give Rani her milk from tomorrow?" he asks, his brow clearing.

"Gladly, Kashi," I tell him, "That is a very beautiful thought."

SISTER ACT

One of the children once asked me whether animals had feelings like us. Well, animals certainly do have feelings although they express them in ways other than words. But do we ever pause to think what goes on in their world? Whether they are happy the way they are? Whether they would like to be able to speak like humans? What they think of us two-legged creatures? Maybe they think we are strange, walking on two legs instead of four. Or maybe they wonder why we have so many problems when life is really so simple. Most of us will never have answers to these questions. But there are people who can actually communicate with these, our fellow creatures. These are persons who are able to transcend the boundaries of language and words. They are so much a part of this life force that they are one with everything. Like Baba.

One of the stories which always delights the children is the story of Baba and the two lizards. Have you ever observed a lizard? It seems to slither across the wall as though in a big hurry and then suddenly stops in the middle of nowhere, deadly still. And then it starts to chirp. Many people believe that hearing the chirping of a lizard is a bad omen.

One day, when Baba was in Dwarkamai with a devotee, they heard the loud chirping of a lizard. The devotee, who was quite superstitious, was at once alarmed.

He instinctively turned to Baba for guidance. "Baba," he said, "that lizard has been chirping continuously for the past few minutes. I hope no ill will befall us."

Amused by the reaction of the devotee, Baba said to him, "Why do you assume something ominous is about to happen? Maybe she is chirping because she is happy."

"But Baba," persisted the devotee, "It is said that hearing a lizard chirp brings bad luck."

Baba's eyes were dancing, but with an absolutely straight face he said, "My son, I'll let you in on a little secret. That lizard is not going to bring you any ill luck. She is chirping because she is excited. She is expecting her sister from Aurangabad to visit her."

The devotee was nonplussed. How did Baba know that the lizard was expecting a visit from her sister? First of all, could the lizard have a sister? In Aurangabad? Was Baba making fun of him? Thinking that he might make a fool of himself, he let the matter drop.

Some time elapsed and other people came for Baba's *darshan*. The afternoon progressed amidst the usual talk and discussions. All of a sudden, there was the sound of horse's hooves. A man on horseback was soon visible. It was discovered that he was a trader from Aurangabad who had come for *darshan*. Deciding to give his horse his feed, the trader took out the feedbag. As everyone watched him empty it, there suddenly dropped out from it a lizard that quickly scurried away to safety!

It did not appear remarkable to anyone that a lizard should drop out of the feedbag. That is, to anyone but the devotee who had had the earlier conversation with Baba about the chirping lizard. His jaw was now hanging open. Seeing the look of utter disbelief on his face Baba laughingly whispered to him, "Now watch that lizard carefully. See how she will greet her sister."

The devotee could not take his eyes off the lizard. He watched in awe as the lizard made straight for her sister who had begun chirping again. The two sisters circled each other, dancing in all directions, chirping loudly and incessantly, their joy visible for all to see.

There was nothing left to be said. The devotee looked into Baba's eyes, mutely acknowledging his intuition and greatness. Who would have ever thought that a tiny creature like a lizard could have a family and feelings and affection? In his simple, unique way Baba had conveyed an important lesson about the oneness of life, the common force that drives all living creatures and the necessity of co-existence of all forms of life. He had explained in his subtle way, how animal life is part of this wonderful creation and therefore merits respect too.

THE FROG AND THE SERPENT

Baba spoke in quiet tones. His low voice reverberated around Dwarkamai in the stillness of the afternoon. There were just a few of us around. It had all started when someone asked Baba about the cycle of birth and death. Did it really exist, as we had all been told so often? Was this birth really the result of good and bad deeds accumulated over many, many previous births? Baba had looked around with a slight smile on his face.

"Our desire to think rationally makes us doubt such ideas, does it not?" he asked. "These are all theories until one contemplates within and experiences that divine power which suddenly makes everything crystal clear. I am going to narrate to you a story just as it happened, a story that encompasses many births."

There was a hushed silence all around. This was one of those eternal questions, the answer to which seemed to be within the grasp of only a select few. But here was our Master, truly a realized soul, who would now reveal some of that mystery to us.

A bee flew overhead, its buzzing distinct in the sudden quietness of Dwarkamai. The crows cawed uncaringly outside, oblivious to the sound of Baba's voice. In the distance could be heard a multitude of sounds signifying a normal day – bullock carts, cowbells, crying babies. It was all in sharp contrast to the special intensity in Baba that day, a desire to communicate something of the knowledge he had.

"One day, as I finished bathing in the river and sat by the river bank in the shade of some trees, a stranger walked up to me and upon greeting me, sat down. 'You are far from the mosque,' he said to me, 'Come, share a meal. You can go back later when the day gets cooler.' As we sat thus, we could hear in the distance the croaking of a frog. A croaking piteous enough to make the stranger ask, 'What is this creature that makes this heartrending sound?'

'It is a frog facing his nemesis,' I said to him. 'His *karma*, the result of his past actions, has finally caught up with him. He is now trapped in the jaws of a snake.'

'This, I must see for myself,' said the stranger, and so saying, went to find the creature. He soon returned, a horrified look upon his face. 'It is a sight unbearable to behold, 'tis but a few more seconds for the frog to breathe his last,' he cried.

Then I said to him, 'Do you think I have come here for nothing? Do you believe the serpent can harm him when I, his father, am sitting here, looking out for him? Come, let us put an end to this once and for all.'

I rose and started making my way through the tall grass. The stranger followed quickly, matching my steps. We soon reached the deadly spot and looked upon the most gruesome sight. The serpent was large and monstrous and his eyes held a desire for blood. The frog seemed almost insignificant in his large mouth, a picture of sheer defeat, not even struggling any more.

As I moved towards them the stranger implored, ' Oh please do not go forward, the serpent is vicious and has no pity.'

'Do not fear,' I said to him. 'The serpent shall not harm me.' I then turned to the monstrous creature and addressed him in a stern voice. 'O Veerbhadrappa, so much enmity even now, after being born a snake? And has this Basappa, your sworn enemy also not yet repented? Give up this hatred at least now and be at peace.'

Upon hearing my words, the serpent quickly let go of the frog and disappeared into the water. The frog too, realizing his narrow escape, mustered up enough strength to scramble off into the thick grass nearby.

The stranger was watching the scene in astonishment. He glanced at me, a glimmer of comprehension in his eyes. 'Please tell me the meaning of all this,' he said. 'Who is Veerbhadrappa? And Basappa? And what is this enmity?'

'Come, let us sit under the shade of this tree,' I said to him. Making ourselves comfortable, we then lit a *chillum*, smoking it alternately.

'Listen well,' I said to him, 'For this is a fascinating story.'

"Not far from where I lived, was an old Shiva temple. It was in ruins and in dire need of restoration. The local populace collected a large amount of subscription and a wealthy man was appointed to administer it. Unfortunately, in spite of being a moneylender he was a miser and would not put his hand into his own pocket. The money ran out when the work was halfway completed. Seeing his reluctance to contribute, the people once again collected subscriptions but it was still not enough. Then a strange thing happened. One night, the wife of the wealthy man had a vision in which Shiva himself appeared before her. 'You are a good woman, you at least rebuild my temple,' he seemed to say. Next morning, she conveyed the message of her dream to her husband. But he, who loved wealth above all else, would not relent, ridiculing her instead. His wife was a simple woman who unfortunately could not influence her husband.

Soon she had a second vision. 'Do not ask your husband for money,' said the voice. 'God needs only whatever is given with faith and devotion, however small it may seem.'

'But what should I do?' the poor woman asked.

'Look into your heart and you will know,' was the reply.

On hearing these words, the woman resolved to take the matter into her own hands. She had ornaments given unto her by her father and she decided to sell them. But this greatly disturbed her husband whose vision was completely clouded over by his greed. He could not bear the thought of losing the ornaments. He convinced her to sell the jewellery to him instead, in exchange for a piece of land. A miserable plot of land it was, waste and barren, unable to nurture even a blade of grass. A plot of land that had been mortgaged by an impoverished woman called Dubaki for a sum of two hundred rupees.

'Offer this plot of land to Shiva,' said the wretched man unto his wife. 'This way you shall satisfy your vision and everyone will be happy.' Oh, how greedy and depraved can a human being get! Hankering after worldly things to such an extent that one cares not for the righteousness of one's actions. Is it not infinitely better not to offer anything than to make such an offering? How then can one not be affected by these same actions? Why then will one not have to bear the consequences of these selfish acts?

The good woman, however, with total devotion and humility offered the plot of land to raise funds for the temple. Handing it over to the temple priest, she requested him to do whatever necessary to help rebuild the temple. The honest priest accepted the land and promised to use it to serve the Lord.

But strange are the ways of the Lord! Soon thereafter, the monsoon season commenced. One day, there was a tremendous downpour and the sky was rent asunder with enormous claps of thunder and lightning. And then, in one fell swoop, lightning struck, fierce and hard, killing the moneylender, his wife and the poor Dubaki. The land remained virtually untouched, in the possession of the god-fearing priest."

The stranger was listening to all this with rapt attention. As I paused to take another puff on the chillum, he said, 'I begin to see the threads of this web, Baba. But please do not stop now, it is most intriguing.'

I went on to complete the tale of these mortal souls, all so different yet tied together by a common bond.

"All three of them were thereafter reborn. The miser was born to a poor Brahmin and named Veerbhadrappa. In this life, he had none of the wealth so coveted by him in his previous birth. His good wife was reborn as the daughter of that same temple priest to whom she had entrusted the plot of land. And Dubaki, to whom the land rightfully belonged, was born a man and became the gurav, or caretaker of the temple. Now, traditionally, the position of temple caretaker is an important one. He is the one who is entitled to the offerings and benefits from the temple. And the wronged Dubaki was reborn as Chanbasappa, the gurav.

I had, over the years, developed a strong affinity for the temple priest and many a long hour had we spent conversing together. He would often bring along his little daughter whom he had named Gauri and the child would run around and prattle playfully while her father and I talked of things far removed from her child's world. Time thus went by and soon Gauri grew to be of marriageable age. The priest was concerned for the future of his daughter.

'I must find a suitable husband for her,' he would often tell me.

'Do not worry,' I would counsel him, knowing already the life charted out for Gauri by her own fate.

And so it happened. One day, a poor, young Brahmin boy came to the door of the priest begging alms. The kind priest liked the look of the boy and welcomed him into his home. This poor boy was none other than Veerbhadrappa, who, tired of his abject poverty, had decided to go out into the world and seek his fortune. What else is this but destiny that he be given shelter by the temple priest?

After a time, the priest came to depend more and more upon the boy and as was bound to follow, decided to marry him off to Gauri. The marriage ceremony was performed and all was well for a while. Veerbhadrappa and Gauri would often come along with the priest to seek my blessings. A few years later, the priest passed away, leaving Gauri the plot of land.

In the meanwhile, Veerbhadrappa was acutely feeling the shortage of money to support his wife and a growing family. He made desperate attempts to earn a decent living but life was hard.

And then one day, fortune turned favourable. The plot of land left to Gauri by her father attracted a buyer who was willing to pay a huge price for it. One lakh rupees, half to be paid immediately in cash, and the other half in instalments. Veerbhadrappa and Gauri were ecstatic! Their joy knew no bounds. It was agreed to sell the plot of land.

It was at this point that destiny once more stepped in. Chanbasappa, the caretaker, came forward to claim his half of the money. 'It is my rightful share as gurav of the temple,' he insisted. Veerbhadrappa would not part with a single penny and Chanbasappa would not give up his claim. They engaged in heated arguments that had no conclusion. Finally both of them came to me. 'Tell us who is entitled to this money, Baba,' they entreated.

I could see before my eyes just where they were heading. I hoped that my counsel would prevail and they would see sense.

'This money belongs to Gauri, who is the rightful owner of the property. Anything that is done without her consent will not bode well for either of you. Therefore leave it to Gauri to decide,' I told them. This greatly annoyed Veerbhadrappa who then started abusing me. He even ventured so far as to accuse me of wanting the money for myself! I felt sorry for him. Poor man, how greed for money can invoke the devil in one's mind!

He then went home and raged at his wife insisting that she make sure the money stayed with them. Gauri, fortunately had been reared by her honest father to believe in doing right and she was greatly disturbed. She then came to me and pleaded, 'Baba, you are my only refuge. I have no one else to turn to. Please guide me, your daughter.'

'Do not fear, child,' I said to her. 'Trust in God, all will be well.'

That night, Gauri had a vision. The lord Shiva appeared to her and said, 'Trust in Chanbasappa and follow what he tells you. And do not take any decision without first consulting Baba.'

Gauri narrated her vision to me and asked me for advice. 'Give Chanbasappa his share,' was my advice to her. This was, of course, bound to enrage Veerbhadrappa. He picked a quarrel with Chanbasappa and then in a fit of rage, advanced upon him screaming abuses. 'I will cut you into pieces and swallow you up,' he shrieked in blind fury. A trembling Chanbasappa came running to me, falling at my feet. 'Baba, save me from this man,' he pleaded earnestly.

'I will not let him take your life,' I promised him. Veerbhadrappa was dragged away and sent to his home.

Later, Veerbhadrappa died an unhappy death and was reborn a snake. Chanbasappa lived a little longer but he too passed away, sick at heart. He was reborn a frog. Veerbhadrappa has been searching for him ever since, waiting to get his revenge. And that is how the frog found himself in the jaws of death today."

The stranger looks at me with great reverence. 'Baba, this story is most amazing. Who would have ever thought these two creatures would have such a history?'

'I have to protect my children from the results of their own actions. I had promised Chanbasappa protection and I had to come to his aid. I think though that I have broken the cycle of enmity this time. Veerbhadrappa has realized that he cannot harm Chanbasappa while I look out for him.'

The stranger and I sat in silence for a while, smoking the last of the chillum. Looking out over the river, he seemed lost in some other world. I, for my part, had a feeling of great peace and contentment within me. Soon thereafter, I made my way back to the mosque. Life had played out its charted course. If only, I thought to myself, man would exert himself enough to understand the meaning of the course that life takes…"

Baba stopped and looked around at our mesmerized faces. There was nothing to say. Each one of us was lost in our own thoughts, minds working overtime, contemplating Baba's words. Questions seemed to tumble over each other in my mind as I looked back on my own life. I was brought back to the present by Baba's gentle voice. "*Karma* exists," he said softly. "It has to. It is the only means of any kind of assessment of our lives. Every action must have a reaction. If we accept that the soul and not the body is paramount, then the soul has to accept responsibility for every deed performed. There is nothing like 'good' or 'bad', all is just action, which, by the laws of nature, is bound to produce a reaction. It is therefore up to us to decide what action is in harmony with universal laws. That is right conduct."

His words echo in my mind even today.

SANYASI OR SAI?

"I am everywhere and in all places and the whole world is with me. I move everywhere and anywhere. I pervade the universe. I am unborn, eternal and everlasting. I am both the visible and the invisible," Baba spoke thus solemnly, emphasising each word.

And we sat around him in Dwarkamai that day, listening, understanding and marvelling at his greatness.

"If he did not have faith in me, why did he invite me at all? He should know that I always keep my word," Baba said to Jog, in response to the letter that had just been read out to him by Jog.

The letter in question was written by Baba's devotee from a place called Dahanu. This gentleman's name was Deo. One day, Deo had decided to conduct a special *pooja* in his home. He had invited over a hundred people for the midday meal following the *pooja*. In his heart he greatly desired that Baba should bless the *pooja* and grace it with his presence. Of course, he knew that Baba physically never left Shirdi, and Dahanu was situated at a great distance from Shirdi. "But surely he will find some way of granting my wish," thought Deo to himself. With great trepidation, he proceeded to write a letter to Baba, inviting him to the *pooja*. How wonderful it would be if Baba graced the occasion, he thought.

When the letter had reached Baba a few weeks earlier, Baba had fondly replied "Very well. Since he desires my presence so much, tell him I will come with two others."

When Deo received this news, he was ecstatic. Baba would be gracing his home with his divine presence. His joy knew no bounds.

On the appointed day, the *pooja* took place as planned. Deo was at peace. Offerings were made to a big fire that blazed in the centre of the room. The chanting of the *mantras* was carried out by five learned priests. The gods were being propitiated. There was contentment on Deo's face. He received his guests with honour, keeping a lookout for some sign of Baba's arrival. He will surely come, he told himself. Baba has made a promise; he will definitely keep it.

As Deo stood at the door, happy in his thoughts, he saw someone approach his house. A figure dressed in the orange robes of a *sanyasi*. As the figure came nearer, Deo recognised the man. "Oh no," said Deo, "That Bengali *sanyasi* is back."

"Is he the same one who came to you a few months ago?" asked his son.

"Yes," answered Deo, "he has surely come to collect money."

"What does he want money for?" asked the son.

"Oh, he was collecting money for a scheme for cow protection and I told him to come back after a few months. I didn't expect him back so soon. Why did he have to appear today of all days?" replied Deo, his face reflecting the annoyance he felt.

By now the *sanyasi* was at the doorstep. "*Namaste*," he said smiling, hands joined together.

"Don't be agitated, my friend," he laughed, seeing the discomfort on Deo's face. "I have not come for the money. It's just a meal that I seek from you today."

Deo felt a huge sense of relief. A big smile lit up his face. "You are most welcome," he said. "The meal will be served two hours from now."

"Very well," said the *sanyasi*. "I have two other boys with me. Are they welcome too?"

"Of course," said Deo courteously. "All are welcome to partake of the *prasad*."

"Very well, we'll be back in two hours," promised the *sanyasi* and then departed.

After a while, the *pooja* having been satisfactorily completed, the mid-day meal was served. The guests were seated and fed to their satisfaction. The *sanyasi* too arrived at the appointed time along with two young boys. They seated themselves and partook of the meal.

After the meal, the guests began to leave. They were offered *paan*, *attar* and flowers, as per custom. The *sanyasi* too bid Deo goodbye after thanking him for his hospitality.

Standing now in the middle of the empty, cluttered room, breathing in the combined scent of incense and firewood, Deo felt strangely empty. He was crestfallen. "Why did Baba deceive me so?" he thought. "Why did he not bless us with his presence today?"

Miserable thoughts played havoc with his mind. The joy of having completed this much-awaited *pooja* evaporated. He felt dejected and sad.

In his anguish, he dashed off a letter to Jog in Shirdi. "Baba did not keep his word to me," he wrote. "I waited for him but he did not enter my home. I had written to him with so much hope in my heart but he disappointed me. Why?"

It was this letter that Jog had just read out to Baba. Baba had a look of sadness on his face. "He did not recognise me," he said quietly. "If he had no faith, then why did he invite me at all? Just because I was in the garb of that Bengali *sanyasi*…"

"He should have known you would never let him down Baba," said Jog humbly.

"Yes, I went to him as promised. First I went alone and I could see that he was upset on seeing me. He thought I had come to collect money. I then went again for the meal accompanied by two others as I had informed him earlier. But," said Baba, gesturing despondently with his hand, "he did not recognise me. Instead, he accuses me of not keeping my word."

When Deo heard about this he felt very ashamed. He had

doubted Baba and had not recognised him. Baba had kept his word, he had blessed his home with his presence and Deo had not the power to see him. He felt wretched indeed! He had been prejudiced; he had known the *sanyasi* previously and had therefore made assumptions. If Baba had come in the guise of a total stranger, he would have accepted his presence. Oh, how fickle is the mind!

It is therefore most important to have complete faith. Faith can move mountains, they say. Without faith, there is nothing. In any endeavour in life, it is important to have faith, in oneself, in what we do and above all, in our *sadguru*. There is a little song that the children and I often sing. As I start humming it to myself a wonderful feeling of peace and gratitude envelops me.

FAITH

Have faith in Him,
He is Ram and Rahim,
He is the only one
to whom you can turn,
When things go wrong
and the road seems long.

Have faith in Him,
He is Ram and Rahim,
He is your one true friend,
A friendship that can never end,
He shall never let you fall,
Ever waiting for your call.

Have faith in Him,
He is Ram and Rahim,
He is your salvation,
Your only protection,
Let Sai be your guide
and in your heart abide.

Just have faith in Him,
He is Ram and Rahim.

CHOR–POLICE

"Aji, please tell us the *chor-police* story," pleads Narsimha one day. The three children have been playing hide and seek in the courtyard at a furious pace. They suddenly find themselves hot and tired and come into my house in search of some cool water. Rapidly guzzling down the water, they wipe their faces on their sleeves in typical childlike fashion. And now, thirst quenched, they want to hear their favourite story.

"Again Narsimha? This will be the twentieth time, I think?" I ask, amused.

"Oh, it is so much fun," says Kashinath.

"Please Aji," adds Saru.

"Very well. Shall we sit outside in the courtyard?" I proceed slowly towards the *khaat* outside, the children running ahead of me, their little legs carrying them at a fast pace. They squat around me, their faces still flushed and red.

"Aji, the robbers were very ferocious, weren't they?" asks Saru.

"They were awfully scary Saru, with bloodshot eyes and long, black beards," chortles her older sibling, his eyes dancing devilishly. Saru looks alarmed and edges closer to me on the *khaat,* tucking her hand into my arm.

"Don't frighten your sister, Narsimha," I chide him gently.

"Aji, do hurry up and begin," says an impatient Kashinath.

"Alright, then settle down and listen. There was a gentleman by the name of Ganpat Kadam. He was a great devotee of Baba. Baba was very fond of him too. Ganpat lived in Nasik.

One day, he was travelling from Nasik to Shirdi, on his way to visit Baba. Now, travelling by train could sometimes prove dangerous. There used to be lots of *dacoities* on the train and people got robbed of all they had in the dead of night. The train moved along, stopping at various stations along the way. It came to a halt at one such station. Ganpat watched as some people got off and others got on. Apart from himself, there was nobody in his compartment.

Ganpat looked out of the window and watched in fascination as a sea of humanity in all shapes and sizes entered and exited the train. Snack vendors sailed passed his window. People jostled for space, babies howled, the guard blew the whistle indicating the departure of the train. And then, a group of men entered his compartment."

"The robbers," whispers Kashinath, his eyes widening.

Saru clutches on to my *pallav,* caught between her excitement to hear more and some sort of unknown fear. I raise my voice slightly, infusing an element of drama into my narration. I can see the expectancy on the children's faces.

"The men numbered about a dozen. They looked around the compartment and sat down in the vacant seats. As Ganpat looked at them, cold fear numbed him. He started to perspire. He recognised them for who they were. They belonged to the Bhil tribe and were dacoits. They were tall and wore black turbans. They had long moustaches that curled at the ends and their dark beards gave them a fierce air. They had a savage look and their eyes darted around the compartment, taking in all the minutest details.

By this time the train had chugged out of the station. Ganpat looked around helplessly at the men around him. They looked back at him, their intention clear in their eyes. He was surrounded by them. It would be a matter of minutes now before he was robbed, maybe assaulted. The dacoits would take his money and his belongings and jump off the train before the next station. Maybe they had knives, thought Ganpat, in fear. Maybe they would take his life too. 'I must not panic,' he told himself repeatedly in his mind. 'Whatever happens, I must not panic.'

And then, suddenly, Baba's words came to his mind. 'I always come to my devotee's rescue, wherever he may be.' Ganpat closed his eyes and started praying to Baba. 'I surrender myself unto thee, Baba,' he repeated silently. He did not dare open his eyes. In his mind, he concentrated on the image of Baba, trying hard to keep himself calm.

All of a sudden, he heard scrambling and scurrying noises all around him. He opened his eyes and looked around in absolute astonishment. He found, to his utter amazement, that the Bhils were all taking to their heels, one by one jumping off the moving train. Those fearsome faces had a look of total terror. It seemed like they had seen a ghost! They were in a great hurry to get off the train and get away from some terrible calamity!"

"Yippee!" claps Kashinath. "Hurrah!"

Saru's clasp on my *pallav* visibly relaxes and I can see a big, sweet grin taking over her face, showing missing teeth.

"Go on, Aji, don't stop now," says Narsimha urgently. "The best part is to come."

"Yes, of course," I agree indulgently.

"Ganpat watched the scene, totally astounded. When the last of the Bhils had jumped off the train, he heaved a sigh of relief. And then…"

I pause dramatically in my tale.

Three pairs of eyes are fixed on my face, waiting with bated breath for what was to follow. They had heard it any number of times before but each time the level of mystery and excitement was the same.

"Then what, Aji?" whispers Kashi.

"Then, as Ganpat sat down in his seat, he had the strangest experience. Right in the seat opposite him, he saw, seated, an old *fakir*, complete with *kafni* and headscarf!

Ganpat looked at him in amazement. Nobody had been occupying that seat until a few seconds ago. And the train had not even halted. And then, before he could even react, the *fakir* vanished! There was nobody there!

Ganpat couldn't believe it. He pinched himself to make sure he was not dreaming. What was going on? First the *Bhils* ran helter-skelter for no apparent reason and then he saw a *fakir* but he couldn't see him anymore. Oh God, was he losing his mind? Or was this all a dream? Ganpat could not understand any of it. He could not make head or tail of this. He shook his head, exasperated at himself. Maybe it was just too much sun that afternoon, he thought. That was it, that was why his mind was so fuddled!"

There are loud guffaws from the children.

"He must have thought he was going insane," says Narsimha, gleefully.

"That's really funny, Aji," adds little Kashi, grinning.

"Yes, it is," I agree. "But I'm sure Ganpat did not think so at the time."

"When he reached Shirdi, he went straight to Dwarkamai to see Baba.

As he approached him, Baba smiled cheerfully and said, 'So, Ganpat, you have arrived without mishap. Safe and sound

– and with all your belongings too.' Baba's eyes crinkled with mirth and he seemed to restrain himself from laughing aloud.

'Were you well entertained, Ganpat? I rather enjoyed being a policeman,' he added chuckling to himself.

Ganpat stopped dead in his tracks. Suddenly, the scurrying Bhils and the vanishing old *fakir* made a lot of sense. He laughed aloud at the memory. He looked at Baba, seeing the corresponding smile on his face. Master and disciple shared a light-hearted moment together. And then, Ganpat was overcome. Baba had saved him. He had answered his prayer and come to his rescue. He realised the enormity of what Baba had done for him."

"And then with folded hands he fell at Baba's feet," says Narsimha.

" 'Baba, I surrender myself unto thee' he whispered again," adds Saru.

"End of story," pipes up Kashinath, smiling broadly. "Thank you Aji, for repeating it. It's the most fantastic story."

GOD IS ONE

It has been raining heavily since last night. The sky is overcast with dark, ominous clouds. Outside, there are puddles everywhere, the streets slushy and muddy. The sun has not peeped out at us for a long time although it is almost midday. The only cheerful event of the day was that school had to remain closed. Narsimha and Saru had run home excitedly in the morning, soaked to the skin. Their joyful, grinning faces said it all! It was a holiday!

That is how the three children find themselves in my house a little later, playing *sagar-goti*, a game played with dry, round seeds.

"Aji, please join us," entreats Kashi, "It's much more fun that way."

"Yes, Aji, do," adds Saru, "Narsimha always cheats." She glares at her brother.

"I do not!" he retorts angrily, "Its just that you don't know how to play."

"Okay, fine, I'll play too," I say. I can't help laughing at their continuous squabbles.

As I take part in their game, I start singing some songs. Soon, all of us are singing loudly, enjoying ourselves immensely. As we finish singing the faith song, 'Just have faith in Him, He is Ram and Rahim,' Narsimha asks a question.

"Aji, how come Baba is called both Ram and Rahim? Are they not of different faiths?"

"Narsimha, Ram and Rahim are names given to God by people depending upon which faith they belong to. But we must understand that God is ultimately the same. You may choose to call him whatever you want."

"How can he be the same and have different names Aji?" asks Saru, confused.

"Hmm..." I say.

"Alright, bring me a coin from that tin box," I tell Saru. She is back with it in a jiffy.

"Well, look at it this way. This is a coin, correct?"

"Yes," she says.

"Look at it and tell me which side you see."

"Heads," she replies promptly.

I turn it over and show it to Narsimha. "How about you?" I ask him. "Which side do you see?"

"Tails, Aji," he answers.

"Right," I say. "Does that mean that you both saw two different coins? Wasn't it one and the same?"

"Aah!" exclaims Narsimha smiling.

"Yes, I understand," adds Saru, nodding her head.

"Children, all these distinctions have been created by man. God is above all this. He just is. He is everything and everything is Him. How then can He belong to any particular faith or colour or creed or shape or size?" I say.

"Yes, that is so true Aji," says Narsimha.

"Do you want to know how Baba once conveyed this to a person who carried such differences in his heart? It is quite a story."

"Oh, do tell us, pleeeeease Aji," they say at once.

"This particular gentleman was a doctor by profession. He also belonged to the Brahmin caste, which is the priestly caste. Now, this doctor was a very religious and good person. He was a devotee of Lord Ram and faithfully followed all the rituals and procedures prescribed by the scriptures.

His friend, who was a devotee of Baba, once requested him to accompany him to Shirdi. But the doctor was sceptical. He did not feel comfortable going to Shirdi.

'Baba has no religion. He belongs nowhere. I find that difficult to accept,' he told his friend.

'It does not matter, just come along with me,' his friend answered.

'Very well,' he replied, 'But I will not touch his feet. I am a devotee of Lord Rama and he is the only one before whom I shall ever bow.'

'Baba will never force anyone to do anything against his will,' assured his friend. 'Do not worry.'

The two of them set out to go to Shirdi. Although they were travelling together, what a difference in the attitude of each! The doctor was uneasy, not certain if he was doing the right thing in going to meet Baba. After all, he was a Brahmin but Baba had no caste or religion. Maybe it was folly to travel all this way to meet such a man, saint or otherwise! His friend on the other hand was joyful, eagerly awaiting the time he would have Baba's *darshan.*

But great are the ways of saints! Baba was in Dwarkamai when the two friends arrived. As they approached him, Baba glanced at the learned doctor, an unusual look upon his face.

The doctor approached hesitantly, unsure in his own mind what to do. He looked at Baba and saw all the things that made him uneasy. He saw a *fakir* belonging to no particular caste or religion. He saw a teacher who quoted from the *Gita* and the *Koran* with equal ease. He saw a saint who did not follow any prescribed rituals at all. All these thoughts were flying around in the doctor's mind. He thought of God, as he knew him – he thought of Lord Rama. In his mind's eye, he recalled the beautiful image of Lord Rama. The wonderful 'blue-skinned' God symbolising all that was pure and perfect.

And then, a strange thing happened. As he looked again at Baba, he could not see him at all! In Baba's place was standing, his beloved Lord Rama! The doctor could not believe his eyes. But yes, there was Rama of the blue skin and pure face. He was smiling and there was a sweetness and gentleness in his expression. The doctor was overjoyed! He rushed forward and prostrated himself before Rama. He fell at his feet and held on to them.

And then, as he looked again at that beloved face, he saw it turn slowly into that of the creedless *fakir*! This was not Rama at all; it was the *fakir* of Shirdi! Or was it? His mind was in a whirl. Rama and Baba, Baba and Rama, they now seemed to be mere names. They were one and the same! Baba was God incarnate, a true Master. Oh, how prejudiced he had been! How small minded!

Suddenly all his earlier beliefs seemed so trivial. God was God, whatever form he took.

His friend who had been standing by was astounded. He was watching this scene unfold in great bewilderment. Why was the doctor falling at Baba's feet? Had he not sworn not to be swayed by Baba? Was Baba not a *fakir* who had no religion or creed? He shook his head, bemused.

Baba was now speaking to the good doctor. 'God *Is*,' he said, earnestly. 'Why classify him? Does it really matter by what name he is called?'

The doctor was speechless. He had been witness to a most powerfully emotional experience, something that he would treasure for life. Then and there, he accepted Baba as his Master, entrusting himself unto him forever."

"Aji," says Narsimha thoughtfully, "Does that mean that all saints are one too?"

"Yes, Narsimha," I explain, "Saints and highly spiritual souls have all reached a very high level of consciousness and they all form part of that spirit. They therefore communicate with each other at will and yes, they are all part of that same force or *Brahman*."

"Aji, did Baba communicate with other saints?" asks Saru curiously.

"Of course child," I tell her.

"How?" Kashi wants to know.

"Kashi, the Masters have a slightly more sophisticated manner of communicating than you and I do," I say, laughing. "They do not need to send letters or messages like us."

"You mean, they send messages magically, without words?" asks Saru intrigued.

"Yes," I tell her, "Would you like to hear another story about that?"

"YES," shout all three. "YES, YES, YES."

With so much enthusiasm egging me on, I begin to tell them about the amazing communication between Baba and another great soul, Sri Vasudevanand Saraswati.

TELEPATHY

"Do you know who Sri Vasudevanand Saraswati was?" I ask. "He was also a great master like Baba. He belonged to that brotherhood of spiritual gurus, one more of those wonderful, evolved souls that this land has produced over the centuries."

"Was he Baba's friend then?" asks Kashi innocently.

"Yes Kashi, in a way I suppose you could call him Baba's 'friend'," I smile. "But they were friends who communicated on a totally different level, more through mental telepathy."

"How did they do that Aji?" asks Saru, quite taken with the idea.

"Let me tell you this wonderful story and you will understand what I am saying.

Once, Sri Vasudevanand had come to the city of Rajmahendra, on the banks of the Godavari. His presence there attracted many people, who came for *darshan*. One of the persons to come there was a gentleman called Pundalikrao, who was a devotee of Baba.

Pundalikrao paid his respects to Sri Vasudevanand and received his blessings. They then engaged in conversation and soon Sri Vasudevanand discovered Pundalikrao's connection with Baba.

He was very pleased. 'Baba is my brother and I love him deeply,' he said happily. 'Will you be visiting Shirdi sometime?' he enquired.

'Yes,' said Pundalikrao, 'I will soon be going there.'

'Excellent,' said Sri Vasudevanand. He then picked up a coconut and giving it to Pundalikrao, said, 'Please offer this at the *lotus feet* of Baba with my love and regards, when you go to Shirdi.'

'As you wish,' said Pundalikrao, bowing.

Thereafter Pundalikrao kept the coconut with him very carefully. Some time later, he decided to visit Shirdi with some friends. Faithfully remembering the coconut given for Baba, they carried it with them.

It was a warm day. The train chugged along, the sun beating down strong on the tracks. They stopped en route at Manmad station. Finding a stream nearby, they descended to refresh themselves with some cool water. The tedious train journey had made everyone hungry too.

One of Pundalikrao's friends opened the bag he was carrying and producing a big tin, proceeded to open it. The delicious aroma of fresh, homemade *chivda* filled everyone's nostrils. Stomachs rumbled instantly. Ah, for some spicy, pungent *chivda*! Delightful!"

"Yum!" says Kashi, his mouth watering.

"Aji, is there anything to munch?" asks Saru, suddenly ravenous.

"Go into the kitchen and help yourselves," I laugh. "There is some *chivda* and *ladoos* too."

They soon return with plates heaped with food, looking extremely satisfied with life.

"Please go on, Aji," says Narsimha between mouthfuls.

"Alright. Where was I? Yes, the *chivda* of course.

Well, the *chivda* was dished out all round. It was delicious and appetising! But alas, it was also terribly spicy. It made the mouth burn and the throat tickle. What was to be done?

'If only we could add some coconut to it, to tone it down,' said someone.

'Oh, there is a coconut right here,' said another.

And before anyone realised what they were doing, the coconut was broken and added to the *chivda*."

"Oh no, was it…?" says Narsimha, looking alarmed.

Saru and Kashi stopped eating and just gaped, their mouths open. Three horrified faces looked expectantly at me, food forgotten for the moment.

"Yes, children, unfortunately it was the special coconut which had to be delivered to Baba. But their intense hunger made them forget that. Nobody realised what had happened until much later.

Pundalikrao was remorseful and agitated. Oh, what a sin he had committed! It was shameful indeed! What was he to say to Baba?

On reaching Shirdi, they went first to Dwarkamai for Baba's *darshan*. Pundalikrao was filled with foreboding. Putting on a brave face, he bowed down before Baba.

At once, Baba said to him, 'Where is my gift?' "

"So he knew there was a coconut sent for him…" says Narsimha.

"He had received a message already, hadn't he Aji?" asks Saru, fascinated.

"Yes children, Baba had special powers and he communicated on a special level with his spiritual brothers.

Shamefaced, Pundalikrao could do nothing except tell the truth.

'Forgive me, Baba,' he pleaded, 'I have made a big mistake.'

He then explained to Baba exactly what had happened. 'I will bring you another coconut to make up for the one we wrongly ate.'

Baba shook his head. 'Nay,' he said, 'nothing can replace that coconut given unto me by my brother. But never mind, what has happened cannot be undone. However, next time, do not undertake to do something unless you are sure of fulfilling it.'

Seeing the understanding on Baba's face and hearing the gentleness in his voice, Pundalikrao felt once more at peace. He had made a grave mistake but he had been forgiven. He felt sure too that Sri Vasudevanand had forgiven him. By now, he must have surely received some communication from Baba. Pundalikrao looked at Baba, a smile of gratitude on his face. All was well and good with the world, after all."

"Wow!" says Kashi wistfully, "I wish I could communicate like that."

"See Saru," pipes up Narsimha, chortling, "That's how I know what is going on in your mind......and you accuse me of cheating!"

An indignant Saru can only stutter and stammer as she jumps up and chases her brother out of the house. Their happy laughter wafts back to me, gladdening my heart with its charming innocence.

KNOWLEDGE

here are many people in the world who gain knowledge through the study of texts but do not seem to make true progress, isn't it?" Saru asks.

"Accumulation of theoretical knowledge without a Guru's grace is like a boat without a sail or a bullock cart without wheels, Saru. True knowledge is always born out of experience. Therefore one must beware of false gurus."

"Who is a true Guru?" Narsimha asks.

"A true Guru is one who signifies the Truth. He is one with the Divine Force and is free from attachment. He can show you the way. Baba once narrated a symbolic story about his Guru. Would you like to hear it?" I ask.

"Yes, please," he replies eagerly.

"There was just such a discussion going on one day - about *maya* and detachment; about the need to be guided along to gain wisdom. That was when Baba shared this tale with us.

'Once, four of us disciples were engaged in debate about Brahman. We all fancied ourselves to be scholars, having completed our study of the scriptures with our guru and gained some knowledge.

Said one, "The Gita says one must progress through one's own efforts, for the Self alone is one's friend; should we then really rely upon another?"

Another added, "One must undertake the journey of life with faith in oneself. Controlling the mind and thereby the senses, one can find the right direction."

The third said, "Everything in life is impermanent, therefore one must seek the Ultimate Reality, which never changes."

I expressed my view, "What is the use of being well-versed in the scriptures unless one can follow them in mind, body and spirit? One must have complete faith in the guru, believing him to be God incarnate and surrendering to him with a pure heart."

All of us wanted to cross the threshold of mystic experience and seek Brahman. My three friends were committed to making this journey by themselves; I yet longed for the guidance of the Guru.

We wandered deep in the forest, hot and thirsty, when we came upon a Vanjari.

"Where do you lads journey to, in this intense heat?" he asked.

"We are in quest of something," we answered.

"And what may be that quest?" he queried.

"It is a quest not to be disclosed," we said.

The Vanjari nodded and then kindly said, "It is not safe to wander thus in this dark forest without a guide but since you are on some quest, I shall not dissuade you. Before you go on, will you not quench your thirst and break some bread with me?"

But we were impatient young men, on a lofty mission. We had no time to spare for an ignorant Vanjari. "Nay," we turned him down, "we would rather go on our way."

And so we marched on, deeper, into the lush, mysterious forest. "The poor man thought we needed a guide," we sniggered. "After all the years spent in study, we can surely find our way in a forest."

But soon, we began to realize our folly. The forest was not as easy to navigate as the pages of a book. It only got thicker and darker, sometimes confusing, sometimes frightening. Starving, thirsty, exhausted, our spirits were sinking lower and our cultivated minds were no longer capable of showing us the way. We wandered aimlessly in panic and then, to our immense relief, found ourselves back in the little nook where we had earlier met the Vanjari.

He looked at us, four weary travellers, and smiled. "Hmm, was it the wrong path you followed? One does need a guide sometimes, it seems. My friends, I am but a simple Vanjari, but I do know that nothing is ever gained without first filling the belly. You feed your intellect but neglect your bodies. What do you hope to achieve? When the time is right to realize your mission, He will unveil it for you and lead you by the hand. Until then, you will only indulge in fruitless search."

I listened to the Vanjari with a gladdening of the heart. He spoke with absolute sincerity; with genuine concern and surprising wisdom.

"Never refuse food when offered," he continued, "come, I still have some bread."

Ego does not release its vice-like grip so easily. My three friends scorned his offer yet again and would not partake of his food. He then turned to me, his eyes questioning. I felt an affinity for this man, who, despite having so little, offered to share it with us out of the kindness of his heart. Is not such a person one who has truly learned something about life, about the Divine?

I gratefully ate the proffered piece of bread and slaked my thirst with some water. As I proceeded to thank him, a wondrous thing happened. My eyes no longer beheld the Vanjari! Gurudev appeared before us and asked what was going on. I narrated the events of the day to him, from the adventure in the forest to the kindness of the Vanjari.

Gurudev looked at us thoughtfully for a moment and said, "You seem weary from your travel. I could lead you to that that you seek. But a quest such as this is fraught with difficulties. One must surrender completely to the guru and obey his word. Do you accept?"

My three friends consulted with each other again. Of what use was their intellect, if they still needed to be led? No, they would seek their own destinies. They went on their lonely, misguided way.

I accepted joyously and stayed back. Gurudev then took me to a well, tied my legs with a rope and lowered me into it. He tied the other end of the rope to a tree nearby. He left me suspended there in an inverted position, careful not to let the water touch me. He went away and returned after four to five hours. He took me out of the well and asked me how I was feeling. I told him I was filled with joy and bliss. He smiled gently at me and led me to his ashram.

Oh, how can I begin to describe that place! It was all I had ever wanted. The veil was lifted from my eyes. I could see clearly the illusory bonds that hindered my progress on my chosen path and I was able to break them easily.

My Guru became my world - my guide, my teacher, my purpose. I meditated upon his form. He taught me to concentrate, to cease the endless chattering of the mind. And finally, without books or rituals, he effortlessly gave me the ultimate experience of Divine Bliss.

Therefore, I say to you, do not be led astray by bookish knowledge and pointless intellectual debates. If you truly seek the Ultimate Reality, surrender to a Guru, who can show you the way. Do not be fooled by one who only dons the robes of the Guru, without any real experience of Divinity. He will shower you with sweet, empty words, meaningless and shallow. Have faith in the one whose words touch your heart, who leads you without ego or attachment, on the true path to Brahmajnana.'"

Narsimha is silent, thoughtful, taking in the meaning of what I have narrated. I let him try to work it out for himself. After a few minutes he says, "Aji, you said this story was symbolic...I think I understand but could you explain it?"

"Of course," I say. "The four friends symbolize the different types of people, with different attitudes in their life journey. They often know what they seek, but they don't really know the way to reach it. The forest is the mind, which must be under control to be able to seek the Truth. Most of us lose our way because of obstacles put forth by our mind. The *Vanjari* is really the Guru, who later reveals himself. The food he offers is guidance and grace. Often, people only see the outward appearance and their ego prevents them from accepting guidance."

"What about the well, Aji? Was tying him in it symbolic too?" asks Narsimha, intrigued.

"Yes, although in Sufi tradition, this form of meditation is also physically performed. It has a symbolic meaning here, being the overturning of the ego."

"I like this story," says Narsimha simply. I leave him immersed in his thoughts, contemplating the mysteries that have fascinated man from the beginning of time.

PLAGUED BY CHOLERA

I have just finished reading a chapter of the *Bhagavad Gita*. I read one chapter every day. Baba had once said to me, "Laxmi, it is good to devote some time daily to reading the scriptures. Why don't you read the *Gita*?" Ever since then, I have been following this practice. It gives me a sense of great peace.

A few paces away from me in the extended courtyard, I see Janki, quern in hand, grinding rice. 'Grind, grind, grind', the rhythmic sound is familiar and strangely soothing. She fills the quern with rice at the top and soon waves of soft, white flour pour forth from the sides. 'Grind, grind, grind', the hum goes on…

It was the same sound that had caught my attention as I walked to Dwarkamai one morning, many, many years ago. It sounded familiar and yet so strange coming from the *masjid*. I was intrigued. Who was using the grinding stone at Dwarkamai and that too so early in the day? It all seemed most mysterious.

I hastened my steps and entered Dwarkamai, eager to find out the meaning of this unusual occurrence. And the sight that met my eyes was unusual indeed! I just stood and gaped! It was Baba himself who was sitting at the grinding stone, grinding furiously like a man possessed.

This was a very different Baba from the one I knew. The sleeves of his *kafni* were carelessly rolled up, its folds tucked in. There was a bag of wheat near him from which he periodically took out handfuls of the grain. The grinding stone was placed on a sack to collect the ground wheat flour. Baba was grinding the wheat vigourously, nay with a kind of ferocity. There was a look of acute concentration on his face, almost fierce, which worried me a little. I hesitantly went up to him. There was no welcoming, gentle smile for me that day, just a brief look and nod. I instinctively sensed his need to be silent and sat down at a distance, watching him expel so much energy on grinding that wheat.

Baba continued ceaselessly seemingly bent on grinding that entire bag of wheat. I looked on, unable to understand the purpose of what he was trying to achieve. After all, he did not need any wheat flour for himself. So who was it for? Maybe he wanted to give it away to someone. But then, why grind it in the first place? The more I mused about it, the more confused I got.

It was a warm day. By that time, Baba was perspiring profusely. But he would not stop. The grinding seemed to consume his entire attention. He did not notice when people came into Dwarkamai. He did not notice them talking animatedly in whispers about his strange behaviour. He did not even notice the four women who walked in and stared at him aghast. That is, until they decided to take matters into their own hands. This was no work for Baba! With them around, why should the work of grinding wheat have to be his lot? Boldly, they went up to him saying, "Baba, this is women's work. Let us handle it."

But Baba ignored them, continuing with renewed vigour. The women looked at one another and then one of them made so bold as to snatch away the wooden peg of the quern from his hands. Baba at first seemed to get annoyed. He resisted, but seeing the genuine affection of the women, he finally relented.

"Very well," he said, a broad smile lighting up his face, "Grind on then."

"Laxmi," he called, the gentle look back on his face, "Come here child."

I went at once and sat by him happily. There was an indulgent look on his face as he brushed his hand over my head. I heaved a sigh of relief; he seemed to be once more the familiar, loving Baba I knew.

"Baba," I asked curiously, "may I ask you something?"

"Of course, child," he answered.

"Baba, why were you grinding that wheat? To what purpose?"

He gave me a quizzical look. "It is for you and all the people living in this village, Laxmi."

"What do you mean Baba?" I asked, incredulous. "One bag of wheat flour for so many people?"

"Don't you worry your little head over that, girl. You will soon find out," he replied, his eyes crinkling as he smiled.

In a short while, all the wheat had been converted into flour.

"There, Baba. All done," said the women, pleased. "What is to be done with the flour?" Their faces were lit by smiles, the joyous feeling of having carried out some work for Baba.

"Thank you," said Baba quietly. And then his expression hardened. In a forceful voice he said, "Now take the flour to the boundary of our village and sprinkle it along the brook. Then let me see how she dares to threaten my children."

There was confusion all around. She? Who was she? And why was she threatening his children? Why throw away good wheat flour? What did the brook have to do with it?

Seeing the hesitation on the part of the women, Baba shouted, "Go! Do it now. I have already crushed her in the grinding stone, she will not be able to harm anyone here."

The mystery only deepened. It was not often that Baba raised his voice. It scared me a little. "Baba, please explain the meaning of all this," I pleaded, clinging to his hand.

Baba's expression at once softened. Holding me close he replied, "Never fear, child. It is nothing to worry about. 'Tis the cholera. I have made sure that evil spirit does not enter our village. She has been ground and crushed into that flour. Once it is thrown along the brook, all will be well. There is no way she can enter our village."

And so it happened. There was a terrible outbreak of the cholera epidemic in the entire district but Shirdi remained untouched. Baba had ensured that the cholera did not get in past our village boundary. All his children were safe. The deeds of great saints like Baba are truly amazing. Having taken on the task of looking after his own, he always kept us out of harm's way. We lived secure in the knowledge that Baba, our protector and master, was looking out for us.

THE TALE OF TWO PILGRIMS

It is a warm and lazy afternoon. The cool interior of my thatched house offers some much-needed relief from the unbearable heat outside. I spread out a straw mat on the floor and lay myself down. I feel a little tired today. I have spent the morning preparing some traditional sweets. I always keep something in stock for my little friends. The first thing those imps do upon entering my house is to inspect the brass jars in the kitchen. I make sure never to disappoint them.

I could do with a slight nap, I tell myself, stretching out peacefully. But that is not to be. Within minutes of dozing off, there is a patter of running feet. And a voice whispers loudly, "Aji, are you asleep?" I open my eyes to see Kashinath's round face and cheeks, his dark eyes staring intently at me.

"Not any more, Kashi," I laugh. "Why are you not taking a nap, child?"

"I am not sleepy," answers Kashi, with a big yawn. "Can you tell me a story?"

"Oh, I see. Alright then, come and lie down beside me."

Kashi stretches himself out on the straw mat.

"Let me see...have I told you the story of Baba and the two pilgrims from Goa?" I ask.

"No Aji, please tell me," he says.

I smooth away the stray floppy hair falling on his small forehead and start to piece together the story from memory.

"One day, we were at Dwarkamai with Baba. Suddenly, two gentlemen arrived and paid their respects to Baba. They informed us that they were from Goa and had come to Shirdi for Baba's *darshan*. They stood before Baba, both of them obviously pleased and happy to be there. Baba then turned to the first gentleman and said, 'Give me fifteen rupees as *dakshina*.' The gentleman immediately drew out fifteen rupees from his pocket and gave it to Baba. Thereupon, the second gentleman pulled out thirty-five rupees from his wallet and offered it. But Baba refused to accept it.

Seeing the crestfallen look on the face of the second gentleman, Shama, who was present too, felt sorry. Why did Baba have to do that? he thought. Turning to Baba, he asked, 'Why hurt this person's feelings Baba? He offered you *dakshina*, why did you refuse?'

Then Baba smiled and said to him, ' Shama, I do not ask for money for myself. What need do I have for it? I only ask to free my children from debt that they have incurred in their past.'

'What do you mean, Baba?' asked Shama puzzled, trying to comprehend the meaning of what Baba had said.

Baba sighed. 'Shama, when people are in need of help, they make promises and vows to God. Then they forget about them. In this way, they accumulate debts. It is then up to me to free them from their debts by asking for *dakshina*. A long time ago, this gentleman had pledged fifteen rupees to God from his first salary if he got a job. He did get his job and salary but he forgot all about his promise. Therefore I am collecting it today, to release him from further obligation.'

'And what about the other gentleman then?' asked Shama.

'Ah, Shama is curious today,' Baba answered indulgently. Baba always had a special fondness for Shama. 'Alright, listen.'

'Once, long ago, I was wandering along the sea coast. In the distance I perceived a large house. Feeling weary after my long walk, I decided to rest awhile on the *verandah* of the house. The master of the house saw me and came out. He proceeded to invite me in and made me welcome, offering me refreshments. Looking around me, I noted that he was a wealthy man. I gathered from our conversation that he was a Brahmin of good ancestry.

He then offered me a place to sleep for the night near a built-in wall cupboard. I gratefully accepted. Fatigue overtook me and I promptly fell asleep. On waking up, I got the shock of my life. While I was sleeping, all my money had been stolen. I had been relieved of thirty thousand rupees! The enormity of this discovery soon sank in and I was terribly agitated. The Brahmin tried to console me and offered me shelter for a few more days. I continued to live in his house for the following two weeks.

One day, as I sat dejected on the *verandah*, a *fakir* came by and saw me weeping. He stopped to talk to me and asked me about my problems. He seemed kindly and I poured out my heart to him.

Giving me a thoughtful look he said, 'Your problems will be sorted out if you follow what I say.'

'Anything,' I answered, my desperation showing clearly on my face.

'Alright,' he said, 'There is a *fakir* who has incredible powers. If you surrender to him, your problems will be at an end. But until you get back your lost money, you must give up an item of food that you are very fond of.' So saying, he told me details about the whereabouts of the *fakir*.

I eagerly followed his instructions and met the *fakir*. And wonder of wonders, within a few days of that, I got back all my money. I could not believe it! I thereafter left the mansion and continued on my journey along the seacoast. I came to a ferry crossing but could not get a seat on the ferry. But fortune seemed to favour me and I finally managed to get a place on the ferry. I crossed over to the other shore. There awaiting me, was a *tonga*. I got into it and came here to this *masjid*.'

Baba finished talking and looked at Shama with a huge smile upon his face.

'Well, Shama?' he asked. 'Is your curiosity satisfied now?'

Shama was still confused. What did Baba mean by this story,

he wondered. When had he travelled the seacoast? He had never left Shirdi in all these years, had he? He looked at Baba, totally flummoxed. Baba's face was grave but his eyes were dancing with merriment.

Shama turned to the two pilgrims. To his astonishment he found them standing with folded hands, trembling, a look of stupefaction on their faces.

'What is the matter?' he questioned them. Thereupon the first gentleman replied, 'Baba is truly all pervasive. He has just narrated our stories to you. It is true that I had made a vow to give fifteen rupees in offering at the temple of Lord Dattatreya if I procured a job. And it is equally true that I reneged upon my promise, completely forgetting about it in my self-absorption. Today, Baba has reminded me of my debt and helped me repay it.'

Shama turned to the second gentleman. 'And that is your story then, about the stolen money?' he asked, understanding showing on his face.

'Yes,' said the pilgrim, 'It is. I shall tell you how it happened. There was in my employment for many, many years, a very honest and trustworthy Brahmin. Unfortunately, one day, greed overcame him and he stole my money from the built-in wall cupboard where it was kept. He stole exactly thirty five thousand rupees. The Brahmin came to me on his own and gave me back my money. The rest of the story is exactly as Baba has told you. I got back my money thanks to the *fakir*. But,' he added, tears freely streaming down his face, 'I did not know the identity of the wonderful *fakir* who came to my aid, until this day. He was Baba, before whom I stand now as I speak.'

He knelt down before Baba. Placing his head on Baba's feet he said, 'Baba, you are truly a Master. I am but a simple, ignorant man, driven by this material world. Please accept me as your devotee and shower me with your grace.'

'Rise, my son,' Baba said to him quietly. 'Follow the path of good deeds and detachment from worldly pleasures. Strive to live a life of righteousness and compassion. There is nothing more fulfilling than bringing joy into the life of another.'

The two gentlemen were overjoyed to hear Baba speak to them. They had received Baba's grace. They went back to Goa, rejoicing in their good fortune, their lives having taken a turn in another direction.

Later as Shama sat with Baba he asked, 'Baba, there is still something I do not understand.'

'What is it Shama?' asked Baba affectionately.

'Baba, these two gentlemen had never met you, not even known of you, why then did you come to their aid?'

'Shama,' answered Baba softly, 'They did not know me but I knew them. I have known them for many, many births past. I have to collect my flock to me through different births. They needed my help and I had to aid them. I always look after my own Shama, birth after birth after birth. That is my promise, Shama. After all, if I do not show them the way, who will?' "

I have been so carried away by my narration that I am transported to another world. A beautiful world of wonderful memories. There is total silence from Kashi. I look down at him and find to my amusement, that he has already fallen asleep, his tiny hand clutching on to my own. May Baba bless him, I pray, looking at his face so beguiling and innocent in sleep.

WISDOM FROM A CHILD

Das Ganu opened his eyes and looked around. The first rays of the morning sun were streaming in through the window. As he sat up he realised why the room looked so unfamiliar. This was Kaka Dixit's house in Vile Parle, a quiet suburb of Mumbai. He had come here just the previous day after visiting Baba in Shirdi.

Das Ganu smiled to himself as he recalled that visit. His mind had been still filled with thoughts of the scriptures he had been trying to interpret. He had been working on a commentary on the *Isha Upanishad*. But somehow he had not been satisfied with what he had written. There seemed to be some verses in the *Upanishad* that he could not completely grasp. There was just something there that eluded him. Das Ganu had tried every means possible to proceed but it seemed futile. Debates and discussions yielded no answers and his work remained incomplete.

It then so happened, that he had the opportunity to visit Shirdi. On reaching there, he at once went to see Baba and seek his blessings. The sight of Baba filled him with joy. And he knew in his heart that his doubts would be resolved.

After a while, Das Ganu said to him, "Why, Baba, do you shower me with inspiration and then make my path so difficult?"

Baba looked at Das Ganu thoughtfully for a moment. "What is the problem?" he asked quietly.

"Baba, you have inspired me to write a commentary on the *Isha Upanishad*. And yet, I find, that try as I may, I cannot understand the subtle significance of some of the verses. Please explain them to me, so that I may complete the work in your service," entreated Das Ganu.

"But that is very simple," answered Baba, enigmatically. "Return to the house of Kaka Dixit and the maidservant there will give you all the explanation you need."

Das Ganu was amazed. How in the world would an illiterate maidservant explain the scriptures? When, with his knowledge of Sanskrit, Das Ganu himself was unable to understand it! Surely Baba was jesting!

But Baba looked directly at Das Ganu, absolutely serious. And Das Ganu was enough of a believer to know that Baba never spoke in vain. He had total and complete faith in Baba and did not doubt his word.

That was how Das Ganu found himself waking up in Kaka Dixit's house in Mumbai that morning. As he stretched, dragging himself out of bed, he heard someone singing outside his window. It was a young, girlish voice, singing melodiously. Das Ganu found himself warming to the sweet notes of that lilting voice. As he listened, enraptured, to that tuneful voice, the words of the song hit him like a bolt from the blue. The girl had perfectly explained the meaning of the confusing verses of the *Isha Upanishad* through her song!

Wisdom From a Child

Das Ganu rushed out, eager to see the owner of this melodious voice. He saw to his amazement that it was indeed a little child, the daughter of Kaka's servant. She was happily singing her tuneful song while cleaning the vessels.

As Das Ganu observed her, he was filled with wonder. Here was this little child, dressed in an old, torn *sari* singing away spontaneously about the magnificence of an orange coloured *sari*. Her song described its gold embroidered *pallav*. She sang with great enjoyment about its beautiful border and all its finery. Das Ganu was stunned. She probably did not have enough food to eat and certainly had only torn rags for clothes. Yet she was singing joyfully about an orange *sari* that she might never hope to own.

Das Ganu was touched by what he saw. He requested Kaka to arrange to give the child a brand new *sari*.

On receiving it, the child's joy knew no bounds. She wore it at once; and on her face she wore the most ecstatic smile. She danced and played and sang in total bliss. This was a dream come true. She looked and felt absolutely grand.

But the next day, she was back at work in her torn rags. Her brand new *sari* had been carefully put away. She looked, once more, the impoverished daughter of Kaka's servant. But something had changed, there was a subtle difference in her. On her face was a wonderful look of satisfaction and joy that had not been there before. Even though she was dressed in a torn *sari*, her desire for a grand one had been satisfied. She was just happy in the knowledge that she possessed a beautiful, new *sari*.

As Das Ganu watched her cleaning the vessels again, humming to herself, he understood clearly the significance of the verses that he had been unable to decipher. It was now clear to him: Everything depends upon our attitude. Joy and sorrow are but two sides of the same coin. It is all in our mind. Everything is God, and God is perfection, therefore everything in life is perfection. It is for us to change our attitude to life if we are to be happy.

Baba had fulfilled his promise to Das Ganu. Through Kaka's illiterate maidservant he had explained the most profound and significant philosophy of the *Isha Upanishad*. He had once again demonstrated the oneness of life. He was one with all, even with an illiterate maidservant. Everybody and everything is part of the one everlasting *Atman* and only one who understands this truth will eventually find himself on the spiritual path.

GRACE OF THE GURU

"Aji, how did Baba help his followers choose the right spiritual path?" asks Narsimha. "After all, the same path would not be suitable for everyone."

"Baba had his own ways of helping the disciple on his path to knowledge. He never gave a 'mantra' or encouraged any sort of austere, extreme measures. His path was gentler, more accommodating. He could judge the means best suited to the disciple and he prescribed simple yet effective ways to god-realization," I reply.

"What kind of different ways?" he asks.

"Well, for some it was the chanting of the Lord's name, for others it was devotional songs and hymns and for yet others, like Shama (Madhavrao Deshpande), it was reading scriptures," I answer with a smile.

"Why are you smiling, Aji?" he asks curiously.

"Because I am reminded of the tale of Shama and the *Ramadasi*. You know, Narsimha, Baba had a mischievous streak sometimes; a good sense of humour, even when he was conveying a message." As I recollect the events of that day, I am in hysterics.

"Oh, please narrate the story then," he says, joining in my laughter, without quite knowing why.

I nod, wiping the tears streaming from my eyes. I try to speak coherently amidst the settling bouts of laughter.

"There was a devout *Ramadasi,* a devotee of Rama, who had come to Shirdi. He would follow a daily regimen of reading the *Vishnusahasranama* and the *Ramayana* at Dwarkamai every morning after his ritual bath. This went on regularly for a long time.

Well, Shama, as you know, was one of Baba's closest disciples and Baba probably felt that the time was right to lead him a step further by encouraging him to read some scriptures. He had decided on the *Vishnusahasranama* for Shama.

Now, you see, Narsimha, the *Ramadasi,* was very possessive of his belongings, especially the spiritual texts. In spite of all his devotion and ritualistic practice, he never parted with his belongings. And to make matters worse, he had the foulest temper. Baba was, of course, aware of that and he wanted to teach him something too. So he decided to achieve both objectives with some light-hearted fun."

I am laughing again. "Aji, go on, what did he do?" Narsimha is impatient.

"Well, the *Ramadasi* was sitting there, reading. Baba called to him and said, 'I have the most awful stomach ache. I must get some senna powder immediately. Do hurry and get some from the market.'

The *Ramadasi* at once rushed to the market to do Baba's bidding.

After he had left, Baba picked up the copy of the *Vishnusahasranama*, from the stack of texts belonging to him. He then gave the book to Shama, saying, 'You must commence to read this, it will help you. There was a time, Shama, when I was in acute trouble. I would not have survived but for this book. Read it at your own pace, it will lead you to supreme bliss.'

Shama was worried. 'Baba, that *Ramadasi* will be very upset. You know what a terrible temper he has; he will surely pick a fight with me. I do not want this book.'

'Leave the *Ramadasi* to me,' answered Baba, his eyes twinkling. 'He has an important lesson to learn too. Here, take it.'

But Shama was not convinced. 'Baba, it is composed in Sanskrit, which I am not so fluent in,' he went on lamely.

'Shama,' Baba persisted patiently, 'you, who are closest to me, I have been guiding for so many births gone. It is now time for me to take you onward, through the means of *Naam*, chanting the Lord's name. *Naam* has tremendous power; it can forever end the cycle of birth and death, leading you to the Ultimate Reality. It purifies the heart and is simple to follow. It has no rituals, no rules but it is sacred and nourishing.

The conscious repetition of *Naam* is extremely powerful, Shama. Repeated without concentration, it will still help you on your journey. Even random chanting of *Naam* is very beneficial. One who repeats the name of God will safely cross over to the other shore, all his sins falling away. The one who constantly has the name of God on his lips is dearer to Him than the most knowledgeable of men. Take this *Vishnusahasranama* and commence to read it.' So saying, he slipped the book into Shama's pocket.

Soon, the *Ramadasi* returned with the senna powder. When he saw that his jealously guarded text was in the hands of Shama, he was furious. He started shouting at Shama, accusing him of stealing his book. 'You are a thief,' he yelled, 'you have had an eye on my book for a long time.'

Shama tried to pacify him but to no avail. The *Ramadasi* went on with his tirade, ranting and raving. 'This was a plot hatched by you to get your hands on it,' he went on, scarlet with rage.

It was comical, Narsimha, the fuss he created over such a small issue. He was so angry, that he was oblivious to the fact that people were laughing at his ridiculous behaviour.

'I did not want your book; it is not difficult to get a copy for myself. And are you insinuating that Baba was a party to theft?' Shama interjected gently.

Baba had been watching this scene with amusement. He then spoke for the first time. 'O *Ramadasi*, can anyone steal the name of God? Does it belong solely to one person? You read your texts every day, maybe know them by heart. Why then is your heart still so impure? What use is all this knowledge if one cannot control one's emotions? A true seeker is free from desire, why then this attachment to some sheets of paper? It was I who gave it to Shama. Go, dwell on the essence of what you have been reading, else your effort will prove futile.'

The *Ramadasi* was silenced. He went away to ponder Baba's words. Shama began reading the *Vishnusahasranama* and in a short while, overcame his lack of fluency of the Sanskrit language and mastered the text. Both men had received instruction from Baba, each according to his need."

"The *Ramadasi* had a longer road to travel, he had to throw off negativities before he could be given the kind of instruction that Shama got, isn't it?" Narsimha asks.

"That's right," I reply, impressed with Narismha's astuteness. "The road to self-realization is long Narsimha, but the Guru can shorten it if one reposes faith in him. Without the grace of a Guru, one has to struggle."

THE VISION

The roar of the sea is deafening. The waves clash, chasing each other at a furious pace, finally petering out on to the sandy beach. I stand still as the foamy white surges of water wash over my feet. They look so tame now, and quiet; making me wonder where all the furious energy has gone. Are these the same waves I saw battling in the midst of that wild, turbulent sea? Appearing out of nowhere, joyously rushing on with the energy of youth. I suppose they don't have a care in the world; they just exist. In the midst of the vast ocean. A wonderful, exciting ocean under a clear blue sky. An ocean offering itself as a playground for all that arrogant boundless energy. Oh, what a thrill it must be to feel a part of that frolic. How wonderful to wholeheartedly expend that force, competing and cavorting with the other magnificent waves.

Do they ever wonder, I think to myself, whence they come and where they are headed? Do they imagine that they may reach a point when that burst of fury will be spent, never to return? Just the way life plays itself out, I muse...

I continue staring in fascination at the sea reflecting the colours of the sky in myriad shades. The untamed passion of its waves is riveting, filling my senses with its sheer natural beauty. So beautiful and yet so elemental, I think to myself. Peaceful and serene one moment, and then temperamental the next, uncaringly oblivious to everything in its desire to manifest its turbulent form.

Standing on the beach, I feel like a tiny speck, a mere dot in comparison to the magnitude and raw power of the elements. The spent waves continue lapping at my feet. I am still lost in my thoughts, watching this inspiring display of strength.

It is then that I notice the footprints in the sand. One solitary set of footprints, which the water has not been able to obliterate. My attention is caught by something about them, something compelling which makes me want to find out whom they belong to. I am drawn to them, almost against my will. I follow, looking into the far distance to see where they lead. I walk a long way, the pull of the footprints like a magnet that keeps drawing me.

And then, I hear a voice. It sounds strangely familiar and comforting. I look around me. I feel like I am floating, flying high into some wonderful world where I have never been before. I am caught in a swirling haze of white clouds. The voice keeps coming at me although it seems nearer now. I can decipher the words too. I almost jump out of my skin. My heart skips a beat. It is that dear, familiar, wonderful voice that I know so well.

"Laxmi, child," he says, "Why are you so startled?"

And then I see him. Clearly. The same beautiful eyes, the same gentle expression, etched into that *kafni*–clad silhouette. A warm sense of peace enfolds me. My joy knows no bounds. Yes, it is my beloved Baba!

"Baba," I gasp, "Is it really you? I have missed you, Baba." I am laughing and crying at once. Tears of happiness are streaming from my eyes. My heart is dancing with joy.

He puts his hand lovingly on my head as he has done millions of times in the past. There is great compassion in his eyes.

"Foolish child," he admonishes gently. "Why have you missed me? I have never gone away from you. I have been with you in spirit every single moment."

"Yes I know, Baba," I whisper.

He stares into the distance wistfully. Looking at the ocean, he speaks, "Laxmi, life runs its course just like those waves you were watching. A short exultant burst and then mere nothingness. It is not easy to be part of the ocean of life and swim through with equanimity."

"Baba, how can a rudderless boat adrift in a storm ever get by with equanimity? One has to have the anchoring force of a Guru like you, Baba. Tell us what to do so that we may live this life the way it is meant to be lived ," I say earnestly.

Baba gives me an enigmatic smile. "It is not difficult Laxmi, if one has the inclination to do so. The first step is the desire to search for a path. A path that will take you towards truth and eventual salvation. But one must feel the need for that from within."

The sea and the waves and the haze of clouds slowly begin to dissipate and I am suddenly transported to the familiar

The Vision

environs of Dwarkamai. And I see sitting there, my beloved Baba. His left leg is folded, the other placed before him; his right hand rests on the knee. There is a halo around his head. He exudes a divine light, like a beacon, a hope for souls struggling in the sea of life.

"Baba," I ask, "You always said that this universe is a *leela* of God. What then is God, Baba?"

"Laxmi," he answers, looking directly at me, "God just *Is*. He is everything. He is perfect, infinite and eternal. He is the one who creates, He is the one who protects and He is also the one who destroys. He is all-pervasive. He just *Is*. Never doubt that."

"And how does one find Him Baba? Where does one look for Him?"

Baba speaks slowly and clearly. "He is within you my child, within each one of us. Seek Him inside yourself, notice Him in every form of creation, develop the ability to recognize Him. He is there for all to see, one just needs the vision to see Him."

"It is difficult for most people to develop such an insight Baba. How can a simple mind comprehend all this?" I ask.

Baba smiles a beautiful smile. "The simpler the mind, the easier it is to find God, Laxmi. Entrust your mind to the Guru, let him be your guide on this journey. And you shall find God. All you need is faith and patience. It's simple really."

"But Baba, living in this world, one cannot escape the upheavals caused by our senses. Grief, anger, greed are emotions that are so difficult to control."

"Yes, they are difficult to control, but not impossible. Even if one does not completely succeed, it is the striving towards that end that is important, Laxmi. The Guru helps you with the rest, steadying you when you stumble."

He pauses for a brief moment and continues, "Perform your duty without complaining, do not speak badly of others, accept your fate cheerfully and do what your conscience tells you is right. This is the first step on the road to finding Truth. And Truth is God."

I listen to his words with joy. Hearing him speak so makes me feel alive, suddenly able to see clearly the path one has to walk on.

"Baba, all this seems so much easier to understand and follow when you are here," I tell him.

"Laxmi, child, I am always here. Remember that. I will respond to him who calls to me. I will communicate with him and guide him from my *samadhi*. I will forever look after my own through endless births. That is my promise," he says seriously.

There is silence for a moment after he speaks. His presence fills my whole being with peace and happiness. I want this moment to go on endlessly, to just stay this way forever. But Baba talks of his *samadhi,* of coming to us from another realm. There is a sinking feeling in my heart. Is he going away again?

"Baba," I start, but he answers my mute question with a gentle nod.

"I must go, child," he says tenderly. "But my spirit shall always be with you."

I put my head on his feet, clutching them like I will never let go. I am sobbing and my tears roll down my face, falling on his feet.

"Laxmi," he says softly, "Look at me."

I look up at his loving face. There is a world of understanding and compassion in his eyes. He stretches out his hand and puts some *udi* on my forehead. "Allah Malik," he utters.

"Laxmi, child, all Creation is one, all souls are one; you are therefore a part of me. Why then, this sorrow? Let not this illusory life fool you, it is all *maya*, an illusion. There is no parting between us today, nor ever was, nor ever shall be. We all belong to the one eternal *Brahman*, that one everlasting life force. The body shall one day turn to dust but the soul shall return once again to live joyously as one with God. You cannot change what is pre-ordained. You can only choose to greet it with a tear or a smile. Therefore do not grieve. Rejoice to be part of this wonderful creation. Rejoice to be a part of God."

…Rejoice to be a part of God…Rejoice to be a part of God…

Baba's voice is fading away. His beautiful eyes are still smiling at me but his silhouette is blurring. There is a faint rustle of his clothes. He is reduced to just a fading outline now and soon he vanishes completely. I hear the last whispering echo of his voice…Rejoice to be a part of God…

"Baba!" I shout, looking around me. But he is not there. In fact this is not Dwarkamai at all. It is my home. I am sitting up on my mattress clutching on to my pillow. The first light of dawn is breaking in through the window. The rooster crows impatiently somewhere in the distance. I have been dreaming. I have had the most wonderful vision of Baba. But it felt too real to have been a dream. I can recall every word and every tone of voice. "Was it just a dream?"I think, crestfallen. "Did I only imagine all this?" I brush my hair back with my hand and sit up with a start. My hand comes away from my forehead with a generous sprinkling of *udi*! My spirit soars once more, my heart dances with happiness, I laugh out aloud with joy! It was not just my imagination after all. I shall certainly rejoice… for being so blessed and having Baba in my life.

EPILOGUE

2003

It is 5.30 am. in Shirdi. The atmosphere in the Samadhi Mandir is charged with emotion. The hall is packed to capacity with devotees. The singing of the *arati* is accompanied by the ringing of bells and the loud clapping of hands. The fragrance of incense and camphor fills the air. The priests wave lighted lamps before the beautiful marble idol of Baba draped in regal splendour. He sits on a silver throne, compassion etched deeply in his eyes and in every line of his face. There is a palpable energy being emitted from the *samadhi*. The seekers stand before him, each one seeing Baba in his own unique way, deriving strength from the experience and belief that when one calls to him from the heart, he will respond. Baba is alive! He speaks from that divine realm where he resides.

The same devotion is mirrored in the nascent temple at Pathri, in the Marathwada district of Maharashtra. It is believed by many that Baba was born in this small hamlet. Here too, the singing gets louder and reaches a crescendo. Within minutes, one is engulfed by a feeling of peace and joy. Baba lives on, uplifting the lives of those who turn to him for solace.

No matter where, there is one thread unifying all these

people - a sincere faith and devotion. Baba left this world to become one with the Eternal in 1918. But one thing remains constant even today – the power of Baba's *samadhi* and the miraculous experiences of the believers. His presence continues to be felt even now, by people in different parts of the world.

A distinguished Parsi gentleman, living in Mumbai, has this wonderful experience to share. The year was 1958; he was a young man whose career had yet to take off. He lived with his wife and infant daughter in a joint family in not very happy circumstances. With limited means at his disposal, buying an apartment seemed a distant dream.

One Thursday, as he was walking on the street, he came across a photograph of a *fakir* on a tree. He regarded it sceptically, clueless about the identity of the face looking out at him. But strangely, something made him say, "If I get an apartment in 15 days, I will look for you." He did not give the matter any thought after that.

Three days later, he received a telephone call from a friend, telling him about an exclusive apartment that was available for rent. Against all odds, the following Thursday, he had signed the rent agreement! It was a dream come true.

"There was something about that apartment," he reminisces. "I often got an inexplicable whiff of some fragrance. And on numerous occasions, I could see a shadow pass by and felt the 'presence' of someone."

And then, late one night, as he slept, he felt a distinct tap on his leg. He woke up and looked around, puzzled. There, standing before him, was the *fakir* from the photograph! He was shocked. The *fakir* smiled at him and said "Beta, bhool gaya?" ("Son, have you forgotten?") and then he vanished. The gentleman was reminded of his words on that Thursday, 6 months earlier.

He promptly made enquiries to find out the identity of the *fakir*. It was Sai Baba. He immediately proceeded to Shirdi to fulfill his promise. This was to be the first of many experiences that confirmed his faith in Baba. "Baba has always looked after me," he says, with tears in his eyes. "I constantly feel his presence."

A young lawyer from Mumbai narrates an overwhelming encounter with Baba at a critical time in her life. She was to appear for the matriculation examination and the work pressure was building. Moreover, her grandmother was in an advanced state of cancer and was going through a painful period.

"My exam was just a few days away," she recalls. "I had been studying late into the night and at about 2 am I turned in. I could not sleep very well and tossed about restlessly. Suddenly, I saw a very bright light on the wall opposite my bed. As I stared at it, mesmerised, a figure emerged from the light and came and stood by me. It was Baba. I was frightened and began to tremble. He looked at me kindly and started speaking to me. He gave me advice on various issues that had been bothering me at that time. And then he said, 'Your grandmother is going to pass away in a few hours. She will come to me. Your mother will have to go away for the funeral rites. But do not worry – I will be with you during your examination.' He then began to move away and I could hear the rustle of his clothes as he went out of the room and vanished. I was in a state of shock. My pillow was wet with perspiration and I could not move. I covered my head with the sheet and closed my eyes tight. After a while, I fell asleep."

Next morning she told her family about her experience. Nobody took it very seriously, attributing it to her nervousness about the forthcoming examination. And then, that afternoon, they received a call – her grandmother had passed away and her mother had to leave town that same day! "It was a very powerful experience" she says, "I felt Baba's presence throughout my examination and passed with excellent grades."

Maria Aragones, a devotee from Barcelona, Spain, writes about her faith in Baba. "Since I was a child, I always felt deeply compelled towards the spiritual. I always wished to meet directly and be in touch with a living saint, to feel the transformation that could occur within me by his presence or influence. This is how I reached out to India and its spiritual Masters. It was the profile of one of them, who loved two religions at the same time, Hinduism and Islam, in its mystic branch - Sufism, that made a deep impact on me. It was Sai Baba. His teachings and character impressed me. I felt it a pity that no publication was available for the Spanish-speaking people of the world to understand Baba's story and teachings. I therefore chose to translate a book on Baba. When the translation of the book was ready, I went to Delhi to meet the publisher. There, at the publisher's office something special happened. The publisher presented me with the English transalation of the great work 'Sri Sai Satcharita', and I felt as though that present had come directly from Baba. The publisher had a painting of Baba, rather big, in his office. Baba in the picture suddenly started to look at me with an unimaginable tenderness, and to shed tears as if he was a fountain. It was obviously a vision that only I could see, and the tears were not material, but to me, the experience was absolutely real. I signed the contract, and while I was speaking with the publisher, I shyly looked from time to time at the picture, that continued shedding tears with a tender emotion. I had to restrain myself from crying. I still cherish within, the memory of that image. Sometimes it brings me tears, and sometimes, unbounded joy.

In Delhi, I also went to the Baba temple on Lodhi Road, where there is a idol of the same scale as in Shirdi. Entering the precincts, I felt that the idol was alive. I was stunned... ecstatic, the Master was expecting me and was welcoming me. That living Master that I had been waiting for was there, alive, completely alive, greeting me and telling me: 'Ah... you finally came!'

I am happy that the book I published has brought happiness to so many Hispanic readers; it makes me feel an instrument of His Divine Grace."

Baba continues to manifest himself in various forms in different parts of the world. Baba had promised, "You will hear me from my *samadhi* and I shall guide you." He has been true to his word.

GLOSSARY

aai	mother
aji	grandmother
Allah Malik	God is the Master
annas	old Indian currency. One anna was 4 pice
arati	waving of lamps accompanied by chanting and ringing of bells
Atman	Soul
attar	perfume
aulia	holy man
Ayodhya	the home of Lord Rama
Baba	a term for father and older or saintly persons
bajri	type of grain
Bengali	native of the state of Bengal
Bhakti Movement	a religious and social movement in medieval India based on love for God
bhakri	unleavened Indian bread
Brahmajnana	knowledge of Brahman
Brahman	the supreme spirit
buddhi	intellect
chillum	clay pipe
chivda	a dry snack of puffed rice
choolah	traditional mud stove
chor–police	a game of thieves and police

dacoit	robber
dacoities	robberies
dakshina	offering made to God and holy persons
darshan	sight of a holy person
Dassera	celebrated as the day Lord Rama defeated Ravana, king of Lanka, symbolising victory of good over evil
Dhoop	village of Dhoopkhed
dhoti	traditional lower garment worn by men in India
dhuni	fire lit by Baba in Dwarkamai
Dwarkamai	Baba lived in the masjid calling it Dwarkamai (Mother Dwarka), the home of Lord Krishna.
fakir	Muslim holy man
Ganga	river in north India sacred to Hindus
ghee	clarified butter
Gita	Bhagavad Gita, the holy book of the Hindus
Godavari	river in western India sacred to Hindus
gurav	caretaker of a Shiva temple
Guru	spiritual teacher
haldi	turmeric powder
Hanuman Jayanti	birthday of Hanuman, the Monkey God
Holi	colourful Indian festival with a fire ritual symbolizing destruction of evil

Glossary

Isha Upanishad	one of the Upanishads – expositions on the Vedas
Jamuna	name of a river
Japa	constant chant of the Lord's name
japa-mala	rosary
Jeevatma	supreme soul
jnana	knowledge
jowar	type of grain
kafni	long tunic
Karma	result of past deeds
khaat	rope cot
Khandoba	name of a god
kheer	milk pudding
Koran	holy book of the Muslims
kumkum	vermillion mark on forehead
ladoo	a type of small, round sweet
Laxmipooja	prayer service to the goddess of wealth
leela	wonderful ways of God
lotus feet	signifying beauty and purity
Maharaj	Master
mantras	chant of sacred words
masjid	mosque
maya	illusion
Murlidhar	one of the names of Lord Krishna
Murshid	Sufi Guru
Naam	name (of the Lord)
Naivedya	offering of food to god during a prayer service
nala	shallow stream

Namaste	Hello
Navratri	The nine days and nights preceding Dassera, usually spent in prayer
Neem	Azadirachta indica. A tree commonly found in India possessing medicinal qualities.
Ninefold path to devotion	The first is Shravan (hearing the attributes, as read or recited)
	The second is Keertan (reciting)
	The third is Smaran (meditating upon the name)
	The fourth is Paadsevan (washing the feet)
	The fifth is Archana (worship)
	The sixth is Vandan (adoration)
	The seventh is Daasya (service)
	The eighth is Sakhya (cultivating fellowship)
	The ninth is Atmanivedan (consecrating of oneself)
Nirvana	liberation to a state of super consciousness
One lakh rupees	one hundred thousand rupees
paan	betel leaf
paat	low stool
pallav	the top half of the sari draped over the shoulder
pedhas	fudge-like sweets made of milk, sugar and saffron

pooja	prayer service; worship
prasad	consecrated food from a prayer service
puntee	little clay lamp
Ramadasi	devotee of Lord Rama
Ramayana	A Hindu epic depicting the life of Lord Rama
Rama Navami	the day of the birth of Lord Rama
Rangoli	patterns drawn with coloured powders
Sadguru	the one true spiritual teacher
sagar–goti	game played with round, light, pebble-like dry seeds
samadhi	a level of very high consciousness. Final *samadhi* is the act of merging with the Infinite, putting an end to physical existence
Samadhi Mandir	temple where Baba is interred
sanyasi	mendicant, someone who has given up wordly life
Shiva	the Destroyer, part of the Trinity with Brahma and Vishnu
shloka	verses from the scriptures
siddhis	Siddhis are yogic powers attained by one who has gained complete mastery over his breath and senses. There are 23 types of siddhis, of which eight are called the 'great siddhis' and are extremely difficult to acquire.

	Baba had acquired all these siddhis. It was with these powers that he could make himself invisible, appear in different places at the same time and be aware of events happening everywhere.
Sita	wife of Lord Rama
swayamvar	ceremony to choose a bridegroom
thali	metal plate to eat out of
tonga	horse carriage
tongawallah	driver of horse carriage
udi	sacred ash from the fire lighted by Baba
Urs	a ceremony to mark the birth and death anniversaries of a Muslim saint
Vanjari	a caste or a person belonging to it - traditionally grain carriers
verandah	balcony
Vishnusahasranama	compilation of thousand names of Lord Vishnu
Vitthal	an incarnation of Lord Vishnu
wada	big house or mansion

Researching the Origins

Shri V. B. Kher, a Sai devotee and researcher, conducted extensive research in 1975 to discover the birthplace and family history of Sai Baba. In his book 'Sai Baba – His Divine Glimpses' he writes, "A man of God, whatever be his caste or colour, is worthy of our respect. In this age of fast advancing technology, when all values are in a melting pot, even every formula of every religion has to submit to the acid test of reason and universal justice if it is to ask for universal assent. Researching into the questions as to the place of Sai Baba's birth, the family in which he was born, etc., may give us a historical hindsight into the later events in Sai Baba's life."

His systematic study of all the available material pointed to Pathri, a small village in the Marathwada district of Maharashtra, as the possible birthplace of Baba. One of Baba's closest disciples, Mhalsapati, had stated that Baba had revealed some information about his origins. Baba had told him that he was born in a Brahmin family in Pathri and had been handed over to a *fakir* as a child. Mhalsapati also noted that when a person from Pathri had visited Shirdi, Baba had inquired about many residents of Pathri by name.

Baba had also mentioned to another disciple, Swami Sai Sharan Anand that he had left his home at the age of eight and come to the banks of the Godavari. Swami Sai Sharan Anand had spent many months in Baba's company and believed that Baba was born in a Brahmin family. Once, his father was suffering from dropsy and it seemed that nothing could cure him. He was keen to bring his father to Baba but was worried that his conservative father might not be willing to meet Baba who was a *fakir*. Reading his mind, Baba at once said, "Am I not a Brahmin?"

It has also been recorded that the well known saint Madhavnath had stated that Sai Baba was the oldest son of a Deshastha Brahmin family of Pathri. When Baba was 5 years old, a fakir had come to his father and asked for permission to take him away.

Shri Sathya Sai Baba of Puttaparthi, who is believed by many to be an incarnation of Sai Baba, has said that Baba's parents lived in Pathri. When Baba was a small child, his pious parents decided to renounce the world, leaving the boy to fend for himself. A fakir found him and adopted him and brought him up until the age of 12.

All these theories suggested that Pathri was the birthplace of Sai Baba. Kher decided to visit Pathri and research them further. In 1975, Pathri was a sleepy hamlet, untouched by technological progress and modernization. Kher made contact with Shri Dinkarrao Chaudhari, a lawyer and farmer from the respected Chaudhari family of Pathri. In one of his conversations with Kher, Dinkarrao made a very intriguing statement. He recalled how his late father had once pointed to one Bhau Bhusari and remarked at the sad plight of a descendant of Sai Baba! Later, some Muslim clients who came to see Dinkarrao stated that Sai Baba had been born in a Brahmin family in Pathri and had been taken away by a *fakir* when he was a child. This would not have been an unusual occurrence. Sufism had taken strong root in this part of India and Sufi mystics were revered by Hindus as well. There were numerous instances of Hindu mystics taking Sufi disciples and vice versa. All saints were regarded as one, beyond social classification.

There were other indicators suggesting Baba's Hindu origins as well. Although Baba dressed as a fakir, his ears were pierced. His knowledge of both Hindu and Muslim scriptures, his insistence on not classifying himself as either Hindu or Muslim, and his reverence for Hinduism as well as Islam, suggest a blend of both influences in his life.

Kher then visited numerous residents of Pathri, gathering all the information he could. He made lists of all the Brahmin families, with details about their sects, family deities etc. From the information garnered, one very interesting fact stood out; only one Brahmin family had Hanuman as the family deity and that was the Bhusari family, a Yajurvedi Deshastha Brahmin family. Knowing Baba's special fondness for Hanuman, it was an exciting piece of information. Interesting little facts soon emerged – there was a 'Lendi' stream flowing past Pathri, reminding one of Baba's 'Lendi Baug' in Shirdi. The similarity in language was also startling. Baba used to speak the same kind of Marathi that was spoken in this area. Kher then visited the broken down, uninhabited Bhusari house in Vaishnav Lane. The thought that this could be the house that Baba was born in was awesome.

He began correspondence with Prof. Raghunath Bhusari, the owner of the Bhusari house who lived in Hyderabad. From the information he provided, it appeared that their first known ancestor was one Konerdada but he had no knowledge of the following two generations. He did, however, provide the family tree of the next three generations.

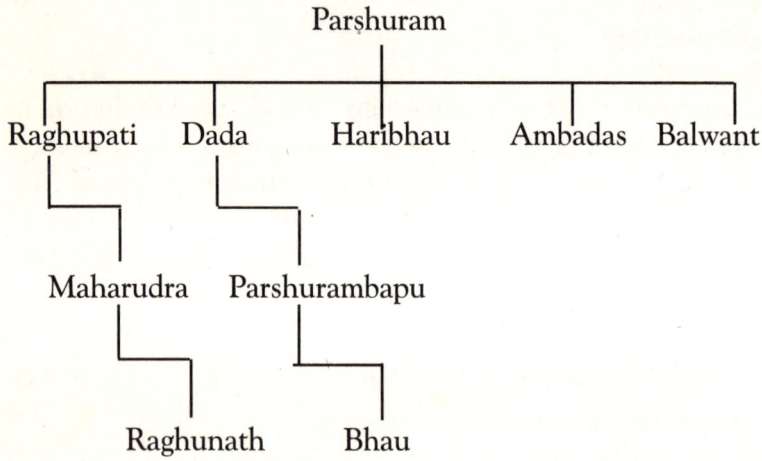

Prof. Bhusari also stated that his grandmother had told him that Ambadas and Balwant had left home to seek their fortune but Haribhau had gone in search of God. In the following generation too, Parshurambapu had spiritual leanings and had taken sanyas in a place called Manjartha, in about 1972. His son Bhau did not do well in life and died in poverty. The comment made by Dinkarrao's father about the descendant of Sai Baba was a reference to Bhau Bhusari.

Could Haribhau Bhusari, who went away in search of God, be Sai Baba? Taking into account all the information available and putting together dates, events and other pieces of the puzzle, Kher felt certain it was.

He writes, "The theory advanced is probable. I discussed it with a reputed historian who agreed it could be so. I do not wish to add anything further. I leave the matter to the readers to judge for themselves."

The Bhusari house in Pathri was purchased in the name of Shri Sai Smarak Samiti and registered as a Trust, with the aim of building a shrine to Baba at the place where he was born. This dream came to fruition 20 years later. On 19th October, 1999, Dassera day, the Sai Baba temple in Pathri was inaugurated. In keeping with Baba's teachings, it is open to all, irrespective of religion, caste or creed. As Kher joyously puts it, "Baba has come home."